Christmas Stories from Ohio

Christmas Stories from Ohio

Edited by Dorothy Dodge Robbins
and Kenneth Robbins

The Kent State University Press
KENT, OHIO

In memory of Ohio son,

DR. JOHN WARREN DODGE,

beloved brother, husband, and father

(1921–1990)

© 2010 by The Kent State University Press, Kent, Ohio 44242
Library of Congress Catalog Card Number 2010008638
ISBN 978-1-60635-064-5
Manufactured in the United States of America

Library of Congress Cataloging-in-Publication Data
Christmas Stories from Ohio / edited by Dorothy Dodge Robbins
and Kenneth Robbins.
p. cm.
Includes bibliographical references.
ISBN 978-1-60635-064-5 (hardcover : alk. paper) ∞
1. Ohio—Social life and customs—Fiction. 2. Short stories, American—
Ohio. 3. Christmas—Ohio—Fiction. 4. American fiction—Ohio. 5. Christmas stories, American. I. Robbins, Dorothy Dodge. II. Robbins, Kenneth.
PS558.03C49 2010
813'.0108334—dc22   2010008638

British Library Cataloging-in-Publication data are available.

14 13 12 11 10   5 4 3 2 1

Contents

Introduction

Dorothy Dodge Robbins

With the first Christmas tree in American history, the creation of the candy cane as a Christmas icon, and the production of one of the most popular Christmas gifts of all time, the Etch A Sketch, Ohio can boast of a remarkable seasonal heritage. The sixteen entries in this anthology, a mix of fiction and memoir, range geographically east to west from the Appalachian foothills to the valley, and north to south from the shores of Lake Erie to the banks of the Ohio River. Perspectives on the Christmas season are as varied as the contours of the Buckeye State. From the heights of elation to the depths of depression, the authors remind readers that Christmas offers a joyous reprieve from winter to many people, but for others the holiday only intensifies the cold and the dark. This collection spans several centuries, from the late nineteenth century writings of Harriet Beecher Stowe and Ambrose Bierce to contemporary accounts by emerging twenty-first-century authors such as Julia Duffy Ward and Rane Arroyo, and offers unique historical, geographic, and cultural perspectives on the season. Sentimental to acerbic, comic to poignant, rebellious to reverent, these yuletide stories and memoirs cover the many moods of the season and explore time-honored themes of Christmas: family, compassion, wonder, and the human desire for connections and reconnections.

The giving and receiving of gifts is a tradition central to the holiday and appears in many tales. While the practice is enjoyable in moderation, several authors warn against excess. Special traditions lose their luster and become routine when repeated daily in William

Dean Howells's fairytale, "Christmas Every Day." Lest we overindulge in the season's plenty, Nikki Giovanni reminds herself and readers that the greatest gift arrives not in a box or stuffed deep in a stocking, but unadorned. Less is more in "Falalalalalalalala," as the poet recounts the joys to be found in modest family gatherings. That it is better to give than to receive is a sentiment that bears repeating in Harriet Beecher Stowe's charitable "Christmas; or, The Good Fairy." And forget department store purchases! In Eric Wasserman's "Early Shnoring on Christmas Eve in Akron," a young married couple discovers that the best gifts are shnored.

A depiction of Ohio in the turbulent 1960s emerges in two bittersweet suburban tales. His hip family's insistence upon updating holiday traditions breaks a young boy's heart in "Blue Christmas," by Robert Miltner, when a plastic tree replaces pine, store-bought cookies trump homemade treats, and rock and roll silences carols. Meanwhile in Cleveland, anxieties about the Cold War cause a child of the nuclear age to question whether even Santa might be a "Red" in Wendell Mayo's "Commie Christmas."

That Christmas, like justice, should be blind is the message in several tales that highlight inequities during the holiday season. Hopes of celebrating "An Old-Time Christmas" are dashed for a mother and her son in Paul Laurence Dunbar's tale about a judge who administers justice without mercy for a misdemeanor offense on Christmas Eve. In "Old Treasures," coauthored by Jane Ann Turzillo and Mary Turzillo, a scrooge of a law officer receives a love lesson from a sarcastic, but blessed, juvenile delinquent. But when a bigoted Santa Claus torments a child too young to read the "whites only" sign in Langston Hughes's "One Christmas Eve," a mother's love offers little consolation. Finally, dismayed at his empty stocking, the title character in Kay Boyle's "Ben" reminds us that Christmas is not just for the young or the privileged.

Other tales commemorate Christmas celebrations and the labors necessary for their procurement and display. In Scott Geisel's "Spring Early," cookies play matchmaker in a homecoming tale that reunites former classmates and several generations. Old World traditions are literally shipped to the New in "A Pig in a Suitcase," Julia Duffy Ward's account of preparing a Bulgarian feast in Cincinnati. In "Ohio Waiting for Camels," the fare is more modest as Rane Arroyo recalls providing hay for the wise men's beasts of burden. And as the lights dim on Rudd Christmas Farm, once the largest holiday display in the state of Ohio, Randy McNutt relays the wisdom of proprietor Carl Rudd in "A Hollow Christmas." Rudd's selfless mission in life was to share the joy of the season with visitors near and far.

Adding a dash of whimsy to the collection are entries penned by Ambrose Bierce and James Thurber. Bierce's satiric "Christmas and the New Year" critiques certain hollow practices associated with these major holidays. With wry humor he deconstructs seasonal greetings and other insincerities. Imitating the terse style of Ernest Hemingway, James Thurber parodies the classic holiday poem in "A Visit from St. Nicholas IN THE ERNEST HEMINGWAY MANNER." In Thurber's revision, Ma in her kerchief seems to know more than the succinct, but dumbfounded, Papa.

This volume offers a double celebration, both of the season and of the great writers who have called the Buckeye State "home." These authors serve readers a varied holiday banquet. The sugar that sweetens the berries is available for the tasting as well as the bitters that mull the Christmas wine. Surprisingly these flavors mix well. So pour yourself a cup of cheer, place your feet atop the fireplace fender, and savor the literary feast in *Christmas Stories from Ohio!*

Falalalalalalalala

Nikki Giovanni

Christmas will just have to hold its horses. I'm not ready. Oh yes, I know everybody is so used to my efficiency that this is shocking news. After all, I'm the one who has usually finished my shopping by late July and am ready to wrap shortly after Labor Day. Have I learned my lesson, you may ask, remembering the year I had purchased and wrapped but forgot to properly label the gifts? No. It was only minor that my father was given a lovely nightgown I had purchased in Rome and my son received a wonderful box of Cuban cigars I had legally purchased in East Berlin, though sort of illegally brought into the United States. Mommy would not have noticed the difference, since she likes checkers, if the whole computer had not come with the game. These things, after all, do happen. No. Christmas will have to wait not because I'm not capable of being ready . . . I have chosen not to be ready.

Let's face it. I was awake last December 26 at 5:30 a.m. anyway. We have five dogs (one for each lap, as my nephew says), and someone has to feed them. I know some folks think dogs lead cushy lives, lying around all day, only really working when the mailman or meter reader comes around, but I don't agree. Dogs have a hard life. How would you feel if you, once a proud canine of the wild who chased his own rabbit for dinner, who reared his children in the collective ways of the group, now found yourself with three old ladies and two boys, or rather young men, whose idea of exercise is turning over a log or two on the fireplace? How would you feel having your world restricted by a high fence with ivy winding its way down, and the cats, who once ran at the very thought of you, balleting along the trellis, laughing at your attempts to get your teeth into them? Now don't get me wrong, I'm not against cats, though it does seem not quite right that dogs have to be leashed and cats run free. But the real question is, How would you feel if you had no discernible reason to be? No real job to do; no place that was expecting you to show up at a certain time and perform a real function? You know how you would feel. Terrible. We know enough about people not having real jobs and how that deteriorates the personality to know that our poor dogs must feel, on most days, positively useless. Yet they forge through, keeping themselves clean and occupied days upon end, watching *Jeopardy!* and *Wheel* and an occasional murder mystery with us. Are they truly interested in these things? I doubt it, but that's their day, and they accept it with a grace we all could learn from. I am still old-fashioned and Southern enough to think living things should start their day with a hot meal, so I am always up by five-thirty to microwave their dog food with whatever scraps I can find in the fridge. My sister, by the way, worries that they will get fat and die before their time; I worry that they will be hungry and kill us before ours.

So I am up in time to make the Macy's after-Christmas sale, is my point. I could, last year, actually have been first or second in line at the door. The previous year I was in the first ten and made some wonderful purchases on wrapping paper, ornaments, Christmas cards, and an electronic pencil sharpener that also opens letters. I have chosen not to go that route again. Am I getting lazy? you may wonder. My son came home from the army to discover I had purchased a red two-seater sports car in his absence. He was both delighted and perturbed. Delighted because, after all, there is a sports car in the family; perturbed because I was not letting, or interested in letting, him drive it. He agreed one morning to go to the grocery store with me because "those bags can be mighty heavy," and as we were trying to get from our side street into the main road I prudently waited until traffic abated. "Gosh, Mom," says now mature but still adventuresome I've-been-in-the-army-two-years son, "you've really lost your edge." Lost my edge? Because I won't go running out into the insane, nay, suicidal driving of Virginia? "Well, I better drive back or we'll never get home." I felt my car give a shudder. I know cars aren't supposed to cry, but they do. Especially when they are purchased by little old lady poets and now know they will be given a real workout by a young man with no regard for payments, insurance, scratches . . . all the things that inhibit mothers from burning rubber. No. I have not lost my edge, nor am I lazy. I just have begun to think that things should be savored, slowed down, really slowly gone through, in order to be enjoyed.

I have traveled for a living most of my life. It's only been in the last few years, after my son graduated from high school, that I could actually afford a regular job with medical benefits, life insurances, and whatnot. I have learned, working a regular job with regular hours in a regular office and classroom, why you need medical benefits, however. My blood pressure, which has been low my entire life, is now up. Seeing the same people every day is really a lot of pressure, but that's another discussion. When you travel a lot you have to get ahead of things, or most assuredly you will be behind. I had to get the birthday cards out early or I would forget; I had to have Valentine's Day candy ordered for my mother or I would find myself in the only town in America that does not have express wire service. I had to have my turkey for Thanksgiving delivered and in the freezer, and quite naturally I had to have everything ready for Christmas or I would find myself on Christmas morning explaining that I meant to get to the store to pick up the wonderful gift that could not be lived without. No more.

Last year we overdosed. Everybody got everybody everything that was ever mentioned. Obscene is not too strong a word. If one more gift had come into the house, we would have needed to reinforce the floor. Did we think the world was coming to an end? Did we foresee some tragedy? I don't know, but December 26, over coffee and the lightest dollar pancakes a sister ever made, we had a discussion. Next year we would make choices. We will have a limit on how much we can spend. Each person can only cook one dish. Is this going to be rough? You bet, because now we all have to think; now we will have to make choices. Yet that is, to me and, really, to the family, the essence of Christmas. Jesus was born to give us a choice; we humans could continue to be controlled by fate or we could accept the Savior and be redeemed. We humans may not always control the circumstances of our bodies, but we can control our souls. That's what is so nice about Christmas. I think I took it too lightly and treated the holiday as a job. Something I needed to get done by a certain time. This year my family and I are getting back to basics. We will be back to telling family stories; back to a half-empty tree with ornaments we have made over the years. The angel on top is the one I made of straws and spray-painted in the first or second grade. We're stringing popcorn and sharing it with the dogs. This Christmas will be our best ever, because we are determined to turn back to the days when it was just us, happy to be together, grateful for the love we share. I shouldn't say I'm not ready for Christmas, because I really am. I'm just not ready for the mall to start Christmas sales before the World Series has been played; I'm not ready for my favorite radio station to start the carols; I'm not ready to be told how many more shopping days are left; and I'm definitely not ready for the arguments about putting a manger scene in some city square. I am ready to slow down and be grateful for all the blessings that have been sent our way. I still like Santa Claus and will faithfully leave him some chocolate chip cookies. Only this year, I am taking the time to make them.

Christmas Every Day

William Dean Howells

The little girl came into her papa's study, as she always did Saturday morning before breakfast, and asked for a story. He tried to beg off that morning, for he was very busy, but she would not let him. So he began:

"Well, once there was a little pig—"

She put her hand over his mouth and stopped him at the word. She said she had heard little pig stories till she was perfectly sick of them.

"Well, what kind of story *shall* I tell, then?"

"About Christmas. It's getting to be the season. It's past Thanksgiving already."

"It seems to me," her papa argued, "that I've told as often about Christmas as I have about little pigs."

"No difference! Christmas is more interesting."

"Well!" Her papa roused himself from his writing by a great effort. "Well, then, I'll tell you about the little girl that wanted it Christmas every day in the year. How would you like that?"

"First-rate!" said the little girl; and she nestled into a comfortable shape in his lap, ready for listening.

"Very well, then, this little pig—Oh, what are you pounding me for?"

"Because you said little pig instead of little girl."

"I should like to know what's the difference between a little pig and a little girl that wanted it Christmas every day!"

"Papa," said the little girl, warningly, "if you don't go on, I'll *give* it to you!" And at this her papa darted off like lightning, and began to tell the story as fast as he could.

Well, once there was a little girl who liked Christmas so much that she wanted it to be Christmas every day in the year; and as soon as Thanksgiving was over she began to send postal-cards to the old Christmas Fairy to ask if she mightn't have it. But the old fairy never answered any of the postals; and after a while the little girl found out that the Fairy was pretty particular, and wouldn't notice anything but letters—not even correspondence cards in envelopes; but real letters on sheets of paper, and sealed outside with a monogram—or your initial, anyway. So, then, she began to send her letters; and in about three weeks—or just the day before Christmas, it was—she got a letter from the Fairy, saying she might have it Christmas every day for a year, and then they would see about having it longer.

The little girl was a good deal excited already, preparing for the old-fashioned, once-a-year Christmas that was coming the next day, and perhaps the Fairy's promise didn't make such an impression on her as it would have made at some other time. She just resolved to keep it to herself, and surprise everybody with it as it kept coming true; and then it slipped out of her mind altogether.

She had a splendid Christmas. She went to bed early, so as to let Santa Claus have a chance at the stockings, and in the morning she was up the first of anybody and went and felt them, and found hers all lumpy with packages of candy, and oranges and grapes, and pocket-books and rubber balls, and all kinds of small presents, and her big brother's with nothing but the tongs in them, and her young lady sister's with a new silk umbrella, and her papa's and mamma's with potatoes and pieces of coal wrapped up in tissue-paper, just as they always had every Christmas. Then she waited around till the rest of the family were up, and she was the first to burst into the library, when the doors were opened, and look at the large presents laid out on the library-table—books, and portfolios, and boxes of stationery, and breastpins, and dolls, and little stoves, and dozens of handkerchiefs, and ink-stands, and skates, and snow-shovels, and photograph-frames, and little easels, and boxes of water-colors, and Turkish paste, and nougat, and candied cherries, and dolls' houses, and waterproofs—and the big Christmas-tree, lighted and standing in a waste-basket in the middle.

She had a splendid Christmas all day. She ate so much candy that she did not want any breakfast; and the whole forenoon the presents kept pouring in that the expressman had not had time to deliver the night before; and she went round giving the presents she had got for other people, and came home and ate turkey and cranberry for dinner, and plum-pudding and nuts and raisins and oranges and more candy, and then went out and coasted, and came in with a stomach-ache, crying; and her papa said he would see if his house was turned into that sort of fool's paradise another year; and they had a light supper, and pretty early everybody went to bed cross.

Here the little girl pounded her papa in the back, again.

"Well, what now? Did I say pigs?"

"You made them *act* like pigs."

"Well, didn't they?"

"No matter; you oughtn't to put it into a story."

"Very well, then, I'll take it all out."

Her father went on:

The little girl slept very heavily, and she slept very late, but she was wakened at last by the other children dancing round her bed with their stockings full of presents in their hands.

"What is it?" said the little girl, and she rubbed her eyes and tried to rise up in bed.

"Christmas! Christmas! Christmas!" they all shouted, and waved their stockings.

"Nonsense! It was Christmas yesterday."

Her brothers and sisters just laughed. "We don't know about that. It's Christmas to-day, anyway. You come into the library and see."

Then all at once it flashed on the little girl that the Fairy was keeping her promise, and her year of Christmases was beginning. She was dreadfully sleepy, but she sprang up like a lark—a lark that had overeaten itself and gone to bed cross—and darted into the library. There it was again! Books, and portfolios, and boxes of stationery, and breastpins—

"You needn't go over it all, papa; I guess I can remember just what was there," said the little girl.

Well, and there was the Christmas-tree blazing away, and the family picking out their presents, but looking pretty sleepy, and her father perfectly puzzled, and her mother ready to cry. "I'm sure I don't see how I'm to dispose of all these things," said her mother, and her father said it seemed to him they had had something just like it the day before, but he supposed he must have dreamed it. This struck the little girl as the best kind of a joke; and so she ate so much candy she didn't want any breakfast, and went round carrying presents, and had turkey and cranberry for dinner, and then went out and coasted, and came in with a—

"Papa!"

"Well, what now?"

"What did you promise, you forgetful thing?"

"Oh! oh yes!"

Well, the next day, it was just the same thing over again, but everybody getting crosser; and at the end of a week's time so many people had lost their tempers that you could pick up lost tempers anywhere; they perfectly strewed the ground. Even when people tried to recover their tempers they usually got somebody else's, and it made the most dreadful mix.

The little girl began to get frightened, keeping the secret all to herself; she wanted to tell her mother, but she didn't dare to; and she was ashamed to ask the Fairy to take back her gift, it seemed ungrateful and ill-bred, and she thought she would try to stand it, but she hardly knew how she could, for a whole year. So it went on and on, and it was Christmas on St. Valentine's Day and Washington's Birthday, just the same as any day, and it didn't skip even the First of April, though everything was counterfeit that day, and that was some *little* relief.

After a while coal and potatoes began to be awfully scarce, so many had been wrapped up in tissue-paper to fool papas and mammas with. Turkeys got to be about a thousand dollars apiece—

"Papa!"

"Well, what?"

"You're beginning to fib."

"Well, *two* thousand, then."

And they got to passing off almost anything for turkeys—half-grown humming-birds, and even rocs out of the *Arabian Nights*—the real turkeys were so scarce. And cranberries—well, they asked a diamond apiece for cranberries. All the woods and orchards were cut down for Christmas-trees, and where the woods and orchards used to be it looked just like a stubble-field, with the stumps. After a while they had to make Christmas-trees out of rags, and stuff them with bran, like old-fashioned dolls; but there were plenty of rags, because people got so poor, buying presents for one another, that they couldn't get any new clothes, and they just wore their old ones to tatters. They got so poor that everybody had to go to the poor-house, except the confectioners, and the fancy-store keepers, and the picture-book sellers, and the expressmen; and *they* all got so rich and proud that they would hardly wait upon a person when he came to buy. It was perfectly shameful!

Well, after it had gone on about three or four months, the little girl, whenever she came into the room in the morning and saw those great ugly, lumpy stockings dangling at the fire-place, and the disgusting presents around everywhere, used to just sit down and burst out crying. In six months she was perfectly exhausted; she couldn't even cry any more; she just lay on the lounge and rolled her eyes and panted. About the beginning of October she took to sitting down on dolls wherever she found them—French dolls, or any kind—she hated the sight of them so; and by Thanksgiving she was crazy, and just slammed her presents across the room.

By that time people didn't carry presents around nicely any more. They flung them over the fence, or through the window, or anything; and, instead of running their tongues out and taking great pains to write "For dear Papa," or "Mamma," or "Brother," or "Sister," or "Susie," or "Sammie," or "Billie," or "Bobbie," or "Jimmie," or "Jennie," or whoever it was, and troubling to get the spelling right, and then signing their names, and "Xmas, 18—," they used to write in the gift-books, "Take it, you horrid old thing!" and then go and bang it against the front door. Nearly everybody had built barns to hold their presents, but pretty soon the barns overflowed, and then they used to let them lie out in the rain, or anywhere. Sometimes the police used to come and tell them to shovel their presents off the sidewalk, or they would arrest them.

"I thought you said everybody had gone to the poor-house," interrupted the little girl.

"They did go, at first," said her papa; "but after a while the poor-houses got so full that they had to send the people back to their own houses. They tried to cry, when they got back, but they couldn't make the least sound."

"Why couldn't they?"

"Because they had lost their voices, saying 'Merry Christmas' so much. Did I tell you how it was on the Fourth of July?"

"No; how was it?" And the little girl nestled closer, in expectation of something uncommon.

Well, the night before, the boys stayed up to celebrate, as they always do, and fell asleep before twelve o'clock, as usual, expecting to be wakened by the bells and cannon. But it was nearly eight o'clock before the first boy in the United States woke up, and then he found out what the trouble was. As soon as he could get his clothes on he ran out of the house and smashed a big cannon-torpedo down on the pavement; but it didn't make any more noise than a damp wad of paper; and after he tried about twenty or thirty more, he began to pick them up and look at them. Every single torpedo was a big raisin! Then he just streaked it up-stairs, and examined his fire-crackers and toy-pistol and two-dollar collection of fireworks, and found that they were nothing but sugar and candy painted up to look like fireworks! Before ten o'clock every boy in the United States found out that his Fourth of July things had turned into Christmas things; and then they just sat down and cried—they were so mad. There are about twenty million boys in the United States, and so you can imagine what a noise they made. Some men got together before night, with a little powder that hadn't turned into purple sugar yet, and they said they would fire off *one* cannon, anyway. But the cannon burst into a thousand pieces, for it was nothing but rock-candy, and some of the men nearly got killed. The Fourth of July orations all turned into Christmas carols, and when anybody tried to read the Declaration, instead of saying, "When in the course of human events it becomes necessary," he was sure to sing, "God rest you, merry gentlemen." It was perfectly awful.

The little girl drew a deep sigh of satisfaction.

"And how was it at Thanksgiving?"

Her papa hesitated. "Well, I'm almost afraid to tell you. I'm afraid you'll think it's wicked."

"Well, tell, anyway," said the little girl.

Well, before it came Thanksgiving it had leaked out who had caused all these Christmases. The little girl had suffered so much that she had talked about it in her sleep; and after that hardly anybody would play with her. People just perfectly despised her, because if it had not been for her greediness it wouldn't have happened; and now, when it came Thanksgiving, and she wanted them to go to church, and have squash-pie and turkey, and show their gratitude, they said that all the turkeys had been eaten up for her old Christmas dinners, and if she would stop the Christmases, they would see about the gratitude. Wasn't it dreadful? And the very next day the little girl began to send letters to the Christmas Fairy, and then telegrams, to stop it. But it didn't do any good; and then she got to calling at the Fairy's house, but the girl that came to the door always said, "Not at home," or "Engaged," or "At dinner," or something like that; and so it went on till it came to the old once-a-year Christmas Eve. The little girl fell asleep, and when she woke up in the morning—

"She found it was all nothing but a dream," suggested the little girl.

"No, indeed!" said her papa. "It was all every bit true!"

"Well, what *did* she find out, then?"

"Why, that it wasn't Christmas at last, and wasn't ever going to be, any more. Now it's time for breakfast."

The little girl held her papa fast around the neck.

"You sha'n't go if you're going to leave it *so!*"

"How do you want it left?"

"Christmas once a year."

"All right," said her papa; and he went on again.

Well, there was the greatest rejoicing all over the country, and it extended clear up into Canada. The people met together everywhere, and kissed and cried for joy. The city carts went around and gathered up all the candy and raisins and nuts, and dumped them into the river; and it made the fish perfectly sick; and the whole United States, as far out as Alaska, was one blaze of bonfires, where the children were burning up their gift-books and presents of all kinds. They had the greatest *time!*

The little girl went to thank the old Fairy because she had stopped its being Christmas, and she said she hoped she would keep her promise and see that Christmas never, never came again. Then the Fairy frowned, and asked her if she was sure she knew what she meant; and the little girl asked her, Why not? and the old Fairy said that now she was behaving just as greedily as ever, and she'd better look out. This made the little girl think it all over carefully again, and she said she would be willing to have it Christmas about once in a thousand years; and then she said a hundred, and then she said ten, and at last she got down to one. Then the Fairy said that was the good old way that had pleased people ever since Christmas began, and she was agreed. Then the little girl said, "What're your shoes made of?" And the Fairy said,

"Leather." And the little girl said, "Bargain's done forever," and skipped off, and hippity-hopped the whole way home, she was so glad.

"How will that do?" asked the papa.

"First-rate!" said the little girl; but she hated to have the story stop, and was rather sober. However, her mamma put her head in at the door, and asked her papa:

"Are you never coming to breakfast? What have you been telling that child?"

"Oh, just a moral tale."

The little girl caught him around the neck again.

"*We* know! Don't you tell *what*, papa! Don't you tell *what!*"

Blue Christmas

Robert Miltner

There was nothing eight-year-old Teddy McArthur liked better than Christmas. Even in the heat of July he could close his eyes and picture an evergreen tree with its glowing lights, beautiful ornaments, and sparkling tinsel, smell the scent of pine and cookies, and sing the words to his favorite songs. Teddy thought that even if you added up Easter, the Fourth of July, and his birthday, Christmas was still better. This would be his first Christmas in the new house.

While Teddy's parents and his older sister Terri loved the new house, he wasn't sure. The suburban brick ranch, with its two-car attached garage and backyard patio, finally gave them the room they needed, his mother said. The extra bedroom was to be a den that could double as a guest bedroom when family from the old neighborhood in the city came to visit.

When asked if he liked the new house, Teddy always said sure he did, but he didn't mean it. He missed the front porches, Mrs. Engle next door on one side, Grandma Flossie on the other, and his cousins, Larry and Tommy, who were close to him in age, just three doors down. He could walk there himself. He remembered the huge silver maple trees on the lawn and the sounds of delivery trucks and fire engines.

But the new house was in a development, the houses were farther apart, and there weren't many kids his age to play with. Hardly any of the lots in Maplewood Estates had trees. The sound he heard most was sprinklers watering the newly-planted lawns.

School ended early on Wednesday. Since it was the start of Christmas vacation, all the children gathered in the auditorium at eleven o'clock. Teddy joined in singing "Oh Little Town of Bethlehem," "Silent Night," "Away in a Manger," "Oh Come All Ye Faithful," and "It's Beginning to Look a Lot Like Christmas." Father Doyle passed out candy canes as Sister Mary Joy led the singing. When they were finished, the Sisters had all the children line up for a drink at the water fountains, then go into the lavatories to wash the stickiness of the candy canes from their hands. *With a corn cob pipe and a button nose,* the boys sang, their voices echoing against the glazed bricks in the boy's lavatory, until Sister Moira called in to them to stop. But Teddy sang to himself all the way back to the classroom for dismissal, *Take a look in the five and ten, glistening once again.*

When his row was sent to the coat room to get ready to go home, Teddy found his winter coat, scarf and mittens, then snapped his rubber boots on over his shoes. He was eager to get home. His sister Terri would probably be in her room, singing along with her 45s. Usually she listened to Elvis singing *Don't you step on my blue suede shoes,* or Chubby Checker singing *Come on Baby, let's do the Twist.* "Even Jackie Kennedy does the Twist," she told Teddy, who replied, "Well, that doesn't mean I have to." The past week she had been walking around the house singing *I saw Mommy kissing Santa Claus underneath the mistletoe last night.* Ugh, he thought. He liked Frosty with his corncob pipe and button nose.

His father had taken the day off work to help set up and decorate the Christmas tree, and his mother had said she would have Christmas cookies ready when he got home. Teddy could hardly wait to walk into the house filled with the scent of ground almonds, vanilla, and cinnamon. Every year his mother let him have the beaters after the mixer had blended the dough, and he licked the knife after they spread the colored frosting on the cookies. In the cold, waiting in line for the bus, he could taste the butter and sugar on his lips.

⬤ ⁚ ⬤

When Teddy burst in the door of the house and entered the kitchen, his mother was sitting at the kitchen table turning the pages of *Vogue*. She looked up, and smiled.

"Hello, Teddy," she said. "Merry Christmas vacation," she added with a laugh.

Teddy smiled back, but something was wrong. There were no wax paper-lined tins filled with cookies on the countertops. No wondrous odor of cinnamon or spices. No oven warmth to greet his cold nose and ears as he removed his mittens, scarf, boots, and coat.

"Where are the Christmas cookies?" he asked.

"Over on the counter," she said, pointing vaguely behind her as she looked at an ad in *Vogue* for Chanel. "I bought a couple of boxes of them at the supermarket. They had lots of your favorites—pressed cookies, frosted and sugared. They even had Russian tea cookies and vanilla bean cookies," she said, looking up at Teddy with a smile.

"But I thought you were going to make them at home. I wanted to frost them and lick the beaters," Teddy said.

"Oh Honey," she answered, "It saves so much time to buy them. These look just as good, and I can make cookies any old time," she added, getting up and bringing the boxes of cookies over to the table and opening them. "Sit down and I'll get you a glass of milk."

Teddy sat down and looked at the cookies. He picked one up. It looked like cardboard. It smelled like an eraser. It tasted like chalk.

"See?" his mother said, pulling up a chair next to him. "They taste just like mine. And no dishes or pans to wash. Just a box to throw away. Isn't it wonderful?"

Teddy smiled for his mother. He wanted to make his mother happy, even though he didn't feel that way himself. He felt like he had the time his sister Terri told him he wasn't a real McArthur because he was adopted. Though he laughed along with her, it wasn't a real laugh and he knew it.

He watched his mother who had returned to flipping the pages of *Vogue*. Her index finger on her left hand was tapping to the rhythm of his sister Terri who was in her room singing along with the radio. *What a bright time, it's the right time to rock the night away. Jingle bell time is a swell time.*

And then he remembered the Christmas tree.

⁕⁖⁕

Every year when the tree was up in its stand, the lights, ornaments, and tinsel added, Teddy's father lifted him up and held him while Teddy put the gold star on the top of the tree. Sometimes he was nervous as his father set down his highball and lifted him. Teddy felt his father's arms quiver a bit as he lifted the star higher, over the top of the tree, then placed it on the top as if it were a cap. His mother and sister would clap and say "Hooray, Teddy" while his father brought him down and set him on the floor, rumpling the hair on his head. *Oh Christmas tree, Oh Christmas tree,* they would all sing, *How lovely are your branches.*

Then mother would bring hot cocoa and cookies into the room. One by one each of them—Father, Mother, Terri, and Teddy—would leave the room, returning with the presents they had wrapped to place under the tree. Mother would turn off the lamps, bathing the room in the glow of the tree lights which reflected off the ornaments and the tinsel. For Teddy, this was the most magical moment of the whole holiday season. Even when his mother pinned Christmas cards to the curtains, Teddy would look at the cards which had decorated trees on them.

"None of them are as good as our tree, are they Mother?" he asked her the day before.

"Everyone thinks their own tree is prettiest, Teddy," she replied.

"As long as it's a Christmas tree, it doesn't really matter what it looks like," Terri added.

His father grinned and nodded his head in agreement.

⁂

As Teddy left the kitchen, he sang *But the prettiest sight to see is the holly that will be on our own front door.* He stopped walking and singing the moment he entered the living room.

There was no Christmas tree there. No pine decorated with lights. No ornaments. No tinsel.

Instead, there was a six-foot-tall silver cone. It looked like it was made from a stick and tin foil. About a dozen dark blue round ornaments were scattered at various places around the tree. It didn't even have a decorated tree skirt. The tree just wasn't real. He started to laugh, but stopped himself.

"What do you think, Champ?" his father asked. He was sitting on the raised hearth in front of the fireplace with its metal sculptures of flying ducks. He was drinking a highball and smoking a Chesterfield.

"We're the first ones to have one," said his mother who had followed him into the living room.

"Watch this!" his father said, bending down near his feet.

Teddy heard a whirring sound and the tree was suddenly bathed in soft blue light. But just as the blue light colored the tree, yellow light appeared, followed by green and red. Then it began to turn blue again.

His father snorted another laugh. He took a puff of his cigarette, looked Teddy in the eyes, and said, "You think that's something?"

He reached near the base of the tree and, as more whirring was heard, the whole tree began to rotate. As it turned in circles, the color wheel went from yellow to green to red to blue.

His father was playing a trick on him, and he didn't like it. His eyes burned and his throat had a bitter taste. He couldn't look at his father or the awful tree.

"What's the matter, Honey?" his mother asked, putting her hands on his shoulders as she stepped up behind him.

"This isn't our Christmas tree," he replied sullenly.

"No, Honey," his mother said, "This is what's new this year. It's an aluminum tree."

"I hate it," Teddy said, folding his hands across his chest.

"Don't be such a square," his sister said from the doorway.

Teddy turned and started down the hallway to his bedroom.

"Are you going to get your presents to put under the tree, Honey?" his mother asked.

Teddy didn't answer. He heard Elvis singing *You'll be alright, in your Christmas of white* as he passed his sister's room. He kept walking.

<hr/>

After he closed the door to the den, he carried the chair from his mother's sewing machine to the open closet and used it to reach the box of Christmas ornaments that was up on the shelf. Inside he found the glass ones that grandma Flossie had given them, the three he had made at school from egg shells, and the reindeer made from Popsicle sticks his mother had bought at a church holiday fair the year before. They fit inside his school lunch box which he had brought into the den. He quietly left the room and went down the hall toward the kitchen.

"What are you doing with your lunchbox, Teddy?" his mother asked.

"I have my toy soldiers in it, Mom," he said. "I'm going to take them out and play in the snow with them."

"Fine, Honey, but don't stay out too long, you'll catch cold," she said, flipping the pages of *Redbook*. "And remember your scarf."

"I will," he said, heading toward the mud room just off the kitchen.

When he was outside, he went around to the front of the new ranch house. There were no trees in the yard, but there was a small evergreen shrub planted near the corner of the house, just past Teddy's window.

Teddy opened the lunchbox. A few snowflakes were starting to fall. Teddy put about a dozen ornaments on the shrub. He had only about twenty pieces of tinsel and he put those on too. Then he looked at the gold star that used to go on the top of the Christmas tree. Because there was not a top to the shrub, he laid it flat on the top, then leaned it against a branch. No one would see it from the street, but he could see it. By the time he was finished, it was snowing harder.

Teddy walked over to the living room window and looked in. He could hear music, *jingle bell swing and jingle bell ring, snowing and blowing up bushels of fun*. His father was leaning over near the fire place, a highball in his left hand, as his right hand lighted the gas log fireplace. His mother and sister moved to the center of the room where they began to do the Twist, their arms moving from side to side as if they were drying their backs with towels. They were laughing and smiling. The aluminum tree was rotating and turning yellow to red to green to blue.

Teddy closed his eyes and the whole scene stopped, all motion frozen. It was like a Christmas card. He opened his eyes. He leaned toward the window. He put his nose against the glass.

A Pig in a Suitcase

Julia Duffy Ward

I don't know what sort of image Christmas in Ohio ought to bring to mind. Snow, I suppose, and we had plenty of it in the Valley. The Valley. How lovely those l's sound—soft, gentle. In the 1940's and 50's, we could depend on snow in northeast Ohio from November to late March and sometimes April. My sister made deals with God before every November 29th, her birthday. What she promised, bartered, traded, I don't know, but generally snow fell hard during the night of the 28th, giving Mr. Roy, the grumpy school bus driver, a few days off.

Being isolated, bound by snow, are metaphors for the years we lived in the Valley. With our move from 19 South Forge Street in downtown Akron to Ira, the Valley's official name, we left the traffic of East Market Street, the houses on Fir Hill with their decaying gingerbread and widow's walks, St. Bernard's Church—its sandstone blackened by soot from Firestone, Goodyear, and Seiberling. We left behind Spicer Elementary School, Pop—the jolly crossing guard, a future at Buchtel High School, neighbor-hood children, the sirens of City Hospital, and Mr. Philby's print shop with its discarded treasure of pink, green, blue, and yellow paper on which we drew horses, castles, cherry trees, and comic strips, and from which we made paper dolls and chains.

In 1950, just before we moved to the Valley, my parents traded in our Buick Roadster. A drive in the maroon Studebaker down Portage Path or Merriman Road, and ten miles north on River-view, landed us in Ira, a span of green between Cleveland and

Akron, where Harmon Cranz planted corn, where his sister Doris and her husband raised a few milk cows and chickens, and where white-haired Miss Clara Belle Ritchie, whose Hale ancestors settled the Valley, arrived from Akron with her driver some summer afternoons, to sit on a wrought iron bench at the edge of a great green lawn to survey the land that less than a decade later she would bequeath to the Western Reserve Historical Society. Childhood was quiet, clean, and green. And, like Miss Ritchie who shooed all children from her property, it was at once oddly wistful and protective.

Mr. Hine ran the Ira post office in the back of his white barn on Oak Hill Road. Our box was number 21; a phone number was harder to come by, though we managed, thanks to subterfuge. My father told the phone company that he needed the line because he was a doctor. Ohio Bell inquired of Mr. Hine whether any of my father's mail was addressed to one. Proof was established, though my father was a professor of English at the University of Akron, not a physician. The ten-party line was a source of amusement to my sister, Elizabeth, and me. We never tired of listening in to Mrs. Knappe's interminable conversations about arthritis and recipes for Campbell's soup casseroles.

This account has little to do with snow or Christmas, but somehow contributes to the insularity—or sweet displacement—I associate with childhood Christmases in Ohio. We had snow and our traditions. Though we knew that there were other ways of celebrating, our celebration became a mix of my father's Dubuque, Iowa, traditions tempered by our mother's Bulgarian ones.

Until we were older, Bulgaria and Bulgarian were just words. I knew my mother's mother, my five aunts, and their families lived behind an iron curtain no one could pass through or get around. I knew my mother had not seen her family since 1935, when she left Sofia, and had little hope of seeing them anytime soon. Their letters, folded into square porous envelopes and addressed in a script so angular my second grade teacher, Miss Kraus, would have frowned, arrived in Box 21. On Columbus Day, when Miss

Kraus invited parents to celebrate the discovery of America, she asked each of us to tell the story of our heritage. I recited her script verbatim: "My mother came from Bulgaria and my father's folks came from Ireland," with little sense of what this meant and, besides, "folks" was a word we never used.

Our Christmas decorations were simple. To see how other Ohioans decorated their houses, we drove to Cuyahoga Falls, where the houses were painted—like Mr. Philby's discarded paper in pastels—pink, green, blue, yellow, and during the Christmas season were strewn inside and out with colored lights. From the first of December on, every house (shaped just like the house beside it) had a Christmas tree, silver with tinsel or blue with angel hair, in a front room window.

In our house, nothing happened till Christmas morning. We knew this was not true in Bulgaria, where the Christmas angel came at midnight, but in America, some time under cover of dark, Santa managed his way down the chimney with gifts, and had trimmed the tree, always real and always fragrant, before we awoke. These were our early Christmases—oranges bulged in the toes of everyday woolen socks—blue or grey—leaving room for candy canes, jacks and a red rubber ball, gum drops and net bags of gold-coin chocolates. There were dolls—a Judy doll, a Kewpie doll, Topsy and Eva dolls; a sled, books, a blouse. One year, Santa gave my sister cowboy boots and guns, and to me a felt cowgirl outfit—with a black and orange vest and fringed skirt.

We spent time figuring out tree lights that all went out when one bulb died, and listened to Ronald Colman's voice on the Victrola, intoning Charles Dickens's *A Christmas Carol:* "Marley was dead to begin with . . . Old Marley was dead as a door-nail." By the time I was ten, I nearly knew the first side of the record, as I used to say, "by hard." I knew, too, that my father would soak a salt cod overnight and bake it on Christmas Eve with bay leaves, slices of lemons, green peppers, onions, and tomatoes, and that together we would make eggnog, beating the whites till they glistened, and sprinkling the snowy froth with nutmeg.

Like Ronald Colman, eggnog, and oranges, Dean Bulger, a real Dean, retired from the University, was part of our Christmases. Every year the Dean came to dinner, dressed in a grey suit, his thin white hair combed carefully to one side, carrying a box of Whitman's Sampler for my mother. Charles Bulger was a widower. He ate my mother's turkey, stuffing, mashed potatoes with gravy, candied sweet potatoes, cranberry sauce, and mincemeat pie along with a glass of Put-in-Bay wine. Soon afterward, my mother would excuse herself, Elizabeth, and me to nap, leaving my father to converse with the Dean, whose eyes my mother said, were failing and could no longer see the accumulation of gravy from past Christmases on his tie. I vowed I would never lose my eyesight. I also vowed that when I had children, I would not nap as my mother did—Bulgarian style—her legs wrapped around mine so that I could not wiggle.

Christmases collected until we no longer believed in Santa Claus, and we decorated the tree ourselves with walnuts bound in foil, and rings of meringue dyed green and blue and looped with string. We celebrated on Christmas Eve, still with eggnog and salt cod. It was during these middle Christmases that Pereskeva, one of a handful of Bulgarians living in Cleveland, visited us for the first time.

Like my mother, Pereskeva was dark-eyed, dark-haired, and she smoked cigarette after cigarette, inhaling deeply, her legs crossed, her hands talking. She drank cups of Turkish coffee and could read our fortunes in the saucers. Pereskeva smelled of rose oil and in greeting and departing, kissed us on both cheeks before pinching them between her thumb and forefinger. She brought us baklava and pomegranates, a fruit that Bulgarians ate at Christmas. Her name was like those of my aunts—Anka, Slafka, Betka, Luiska, Nikolinka—and difficult to remember. She called my mother Marta, not Martha. Her voice, like my mother's, was dark and full. When she spoke to us, she rolled her r's and spurned the conditional. When she spoke to my mother, we understood nothing. Neither did my father, who sat a while on his red leather chair, patiently smoking his pipe, and then excused himself to grade some papers.

Pereskeva was exotic, like the Christmas pomegranates she brought and which we later ate over the kitchen sink. These our mother cut in half, and we ate them as she had in Sofia, spitting the bitter seeds onto the porcelain, burying our noses in the gelatinous flesh, while the juice ran red down our chins. They were a tradition in a country where the valleys were full of roses in the summer, and where, in the winter, the Christmas angel's arrival was announced by a ringing bell. From Pereskeva, we learned it was a country where Christmas was celebrated with a pig—a whole pig with a head, feet, and tail.

By the Christmas of 1971, my father's last, I had long left the Valley. Those snowbound Christmases had become the Christmas stories I told my small children, embellished tales of trudging across Harmon Cranz's corn field with Elizabeth through heavy snow to collect raw milk, eggs, and freshly strangled chickens from Doris Wetmore. I described their Grandmother Martha plucking and singeing our dinner and turning milk into yogurt. I told them about Dean Bulger and Pereskeva and pomegranates.

In the mid-Sixties, my life had begun to stretch slowly beyond the Valley. I went west to study in St. Louis, where I met and later married a cowboy turned engineer, the first Idahoan I ever knew. With him, I saw things I'd only heard or read about—chaps, spurs, cloudless skies, ditch irrigation, sage brush, and tumbleweed. He introduced me to his out-west family, to paying for a turquoise ring with silver dollars, to the Rocky, Blue, and Steen Mountain Ranges, the Snake River, the high plains, and deserts. It was on the Whitehorse Ranch at the edge of the Alvord Desert, where he once worked, that I watched (albeit reluctantly) a cow being shot through the head. A few evenings later, on a night when the Western sky was full of stars so large and bright I knew I could touch them, we were served the steak.

In the years that followed, I traded Mr. Szalay's sweet corn from near-by Everett on the Cuyahoga River for the charcoal roasted ears we bought from vendors along the Bosphorus, in Bebek, where we were living and teaching at Robert College. I traded my mother's Kentucky Wonder beans for fuzzy, pencil-thin fava beans that turned my hands henna-colored when I learned to cook them in olive oil. They were a spring delight in Turkey, where they were served with garlic-flavored yogurt.

I traded springs in the Valley—woodland floors of spring beauties, bloodroot, trillium, and jack-in-the-pulpits—for the view from our apartment, the hills of Anatolia with stately stands of Cypress and masses of purpling Judas trees. Doris Wetmore's chickens were replaced by sheep, their flanks stained pink, to be sacrificed at Kurban Bayrami—a knife to their throats—on Istanbul's streets.

When, after three years, we returned to the US, but this time to southern Ohio, we looked forward to what my mother proclaimed would be a Christmas to remember, a real Bulgarian Christmas. Just how it would be remembered was something none of us could have anticipated. The Christmas of 1971 began and ended with a suckling pig. My mother said she would bring it.

My husband protested, but I knew we had as little chance of escaping a suckling pig for dinner as I'd had of freeing my legs from my mother's during those naps that followed Christmas turkey and mashed potatoes. I understood my mother's longing for a Bulgarian Christmas, and I wanted it to be perfect.

The negotiations, the trades, the bargains began. My husband and I agreed there would be no Christmas angel. Santa would descend our chimney the American way, put up the tree next to the fireplace in the living room, and leave the presents. We would include my husband's Idaho tradition, placing a slice of homemade fruitcake and a tangerine for Santa on the mantel. On Christmas Eve, there would be salt cod and eggnog, and on Christmas Day, mashed potatoes, green beans, cranberry sauce, baklava, a citrus salad glistening with pomegranate seeds, and a suckling pig.

Despite our best intentions, the pig cast a pall over our preparations. My husband was uneasy. He, who had grown up in the wilderness area of Central Idaho hunting for sage hens, ducks, quail, geese, antelope and elk, who had slaughtered cows, had misgivings when it came to his young sons being served a whole pig on a platter. Still, Christmas is a time of peace and goodwill. We were resolved (or resigned) to abide by our agreement.

When the TWA flight landed at the Cincinnati airport, none of us knew what lay ahead. As my parents made their way down the jetway, we scarcely saw them. Our eyes were on my mother's suitcase. We knew the pig was inside.

Memory plays tricks, but this is what I remember. Once home, we carried the suitcase to the kitchen and placed it on the round copper table. The children had been put in my father's care in the living room, where he would tell them the story of old Scrooge's redemption. As my mother and I lifted the green lid of the suitcase, I was surprised by how much room that pig commanded and by how much it looked like a pig—fat, faintly pink, with a sizeable, wrinkled snout. Fortunately, its eyes were closed—or perhaps there were no eyes between those narrow lids. The tail was a stiff semi-circle and the feet reminded me of the jars of pickled pigs' feet my mother kept in her refrigerator and claimed to be delicious. The ears sagged, as though in defeat.

My impression was that the suitcase was very small and the pig was very large. This was my husband's impression too. As he headed to the basement for his steel measuring tape, my mother got out two cookbooks she had decided to bring at the last minute. One was the familiar teal-covered *Victory Cookbook,* the 1943 wartime edition. It contained recipes for boiled or pickled pigs' feet and headcheese, made with a pig's head and tongue.

The 1953 edition of *The Joy of Cooking* (discarded by the Akron Public Library, where my mother worked on the bookmobile) was more helpful. We turned to page 365. Rombauer and Becker begin their instructions for roasting a pig by saying: "This recipe for the old-fashioned way of cooking a young pig is given because it is pleasant to preserve traditional rules."

As I read on, the words "pleasant" and "traditional" stayed with me. We learned that we should neither baste nor cover the pig, but dress it by "drawing, scraping, and cleaning." After following directions for a simple bread stuffing, we were to sew up the pig and prop open its mouth with a block of wood. (For what, I wondered? The apple?) We were to skewer the legs "into position," the forelegs would point forward, the hind legs backward. The pig's ears were to be covered with well-greased paper, secured with paper clips.

From the living room, I could hear my father's voice. He was telling the children about the ghost of Christmas Past. I wondered how long it would be before he came to Scrooge's joyous awakening on Christmas Day when he opens his bedroom window and shouts to the boy on the street below, asking him to buy the turkey in the butcher's window for Bob Cratchit and Tiny Tim. I could hear the high-pitched exchange of the old 78 recording, the incredulous boy crying out, "What? The turkey as big as me?" And Scrooge's reply, "Delightful boy!"

We read on. Rombauer and Becker told us to remove the paper from the pig's ears for the last thirty minutes of roasting. My mother interjected that the ears were crispy, the best part—like chicken wings. Before serving, we were to remove the block of wood from the pig's mouth and replace it with a small lemon, apple or carrot. For eyes, we could use raisins or cranberries. And around the pig's neck, the editors suggested a wreath of small green leaves. What kind of green leaves, I wondered, would I find in Ohio in the dead of winter? I studied the poor pig. Hadn't the Greeks and Romans encircled the heads of emperors, conquering heroes, and poets with laurel leaves?

For a moment, I found this prospect quite bizarre—to dress a dead pig in this way—but exciting all the same. I could see the pig, perfectly roasted . . . I could smell it, too. The skin would be chestnut brown, crisp, crackling. The flesh, succulent. The aroma would be many times more enticing than a turkey's. This would be a significant undertaking. Thinking in metaphors was hazardous. It was a stretch, I knew, but wasn't this a bit like William Carlos Williams' red wheel barrow glazed with rain water? Christmas depended on this suckling pig, and we hadn't yet read about a glaze.

My efficient husband measured the pig. Then he measured the width of the oven, and measured the pig again. And then he measured the depth of the oven, the diagonal measurement of the oven. This was no suckling pig. No oven in Oxford, Ohio could accommodate it. Perhaps this explained why Pereskeva had told us that early on Christmas morning, Bulgarian housewives sent pigs to the baker to be roasted.

The grisly beheading fell to my husband, the man who had dropped out of medical school a few years before we met because he could not bring himself to dissect a cadaver. I imagined the pig on our dining room table between two silver candlesticks. Many scenarios occurred to me. The most hopeful was that at first glance, the headless pig might resemble a 25-pound turkey.

It would be nice to pretend that all went well. It would be nice to say that in spite of everything, the pig was presented (or disguised), wreathed in laurel leaves and garnished with any of Rombauer and Becker's suggestions—baked apples filled with sweet potatoes or mincemeat, or baked tomatoes filled with pineapple. It would be nice to say that suckling pig became a family tradition. Instead, the poor beheaded pig was cut up in the kitchen ("carved" sounds pretentious and "butchered," though closer to the truth, sounds merciless) and arrived at the table looking, smelling, and tasting like sliced pork.

There's no way around it. What good is a suckling pig without its head? The Christmas of 1971 is the Christmas no one spoke of for many years. It was not associated with a delicious meal or peace or good will. Decades have passed, and as is true of family stories, the story of the suckling pig has improved with time and retelling. It has gone from being painful, to memorable, to pleasant, to funny, to downright mirthful. But at the time, my husband blamed me for indulging my mother; I blamed him for being a bad sport; my mother blamed the Akron butcher and all America for not knowing how young a suckling pig should be.

One Christmas Eve

Langston Hughes

Standing over the hot stove cooking supper, the colored maid, Arcie, was very tired. Between meals today, she had cleaned the whole house for the white family she worked for, getting ready for Christmas tomorrow. Now her back ached and her head felt faint from sheer fatigue. Well, she would be off in a little while, if only the Missus and her children would come on home to dinner. They were out shopping for more things for the tree which stood all ready, tinsel-hung and lovely in the living room, waiting for its candles to be lighted.

Arcie wished she could afford a tree for Joe. He'd never had one yet, and it's nice to have such things when you're little. Joe was five, going on six. Arcie, looking at the roast in the white folks' oven, wondered how much she could afford to spend tonight on toys. She only got seven dollars a week, and four of that went for her room and the landlady's daily looking after Joe while Arcie was at work.

"Lord, it's more'n a notion raisin' a child," she thought.

She looked at the clock on the kitchen table. After seven. What made white folks so darned inconsiderate? Why didn't they come on home here to supper? They knew she wanted to get off before all the stores closed. She wouldn't have time to buy Joe nothin' if they didn't hurry. And her landlady probably wanting to go out and shop, too, and not be bothered with little Joe.

"Dog gone it!" Arcie said to herself. "If I just had my money, I might leave the supper on the stove for 'em. I just got to get to the stores fo' they close." But she hadn't been paid for the week yet. The missus had promised to pay her Christmas Eve, a day or so ahead of time.

Arcie heard a door slam and talking and laughter in the front of the house. She went in and saw the Missus and her kids shaking snow off their coats.

"Umm-mm! It's swell for Christmas Eve," one of the kids said to Arcie. "It's snowin' like the deuce, and mother came near driving through a stop light. Can't hardly see for the snow. It's swell!"

"Supper's ready," Arcie said. She was thinking how her shoes weren't very good for walking in snow.

It seemed like the white folks took as long as they could to eat that evening. While Arcie was washing dishes, the Missus came out with her money.

"Arcie," the Missus said, "I'm so sorry, but would you mind if I just gave you five dollars tonight? The children have made me run short of change, buying presents and all."

"I'd like to have seven," Arcie said. "I needs it."

"Well, I just haven't got seven," the Missus said. "I didn't know you'd want all your money before the end of the week, anyhow. I just haven't got it to spare."

Arcie took five. Coming out of the hot kitchen, she wrapped up as well as she could and hurried by the house where she roomed to get little Joe. At least he could look at the Christmas trees in the windows downtown.

The landlady, a big light yellow woman, was in a bad humor. She said to Arcie, "I thought you was comin' home early and get this child. I guess you know I want to go out, too, once in awhile."

Arcie didn't say anything for, if she had, she knew the landlady would probably throw it up to her that she wasn't getting paid to look after a child both night and day.

"Come on, Joe," Arcie said to her son, "let's us go in the street."

"I hears they got a Santa Claus down town," Joe said, wriggling into his worn little coat. "I wants to see him."

"Don't know 'bout that," his mother said, "but hurry up and get your rubbers on. Stores'll all be closed directly."

It was six or eight blocks downtown. They trudged along through the falling snow, both of them a little cold. But the snow was pretty!

The main street was hung with bright red and blue lights. In front of the City Hall there was a Christmas tree—but it didn't have no presents on it, only lights. In the store windows there were lots of toys—for sale.

Joe kept on saying, "Mama, I want . . ."

But mama kept walking ahead. It was nearly ten, when the stores were due to close, and Arcie wanted to get Joe some cheap gloves and something to keep him warm, as well as a toy or two. She thought she might come across a rummage sale where they had children's clothes. And in the ten-cent store, she could get some toys.

"O-oo! Lookee . . . ," little Joe kept saying, and pointing at things in the windows. How warm and pretty the lights were, and the shops, and the electric signs through the snow.

It took Arcie more than a dollar to get Joe's mittens and things he needed. In the A & P Arcie bought a big box of hard candies for 49¢. And then she guided Joe through the crowd on the street until they came to the dime store. Near the ten-cent store they passed a moving picture theatre. Joe said he wanted to go in and see the movies.

Arcie said, "Ump-un! No, child! This ain't Baltimore where they have shows for colored, too. In these here small towns, they don't let colored folks in. We can't go in there."

"Oh," said little Joe.

In the ten-cent store, there was an awful crowd. Arcie told Joe to stand outside and wait for her. Keeping hold of him in the crowded store would be a job. Besides she didn't want him to see what toys she was buying. They were to be a surprise from Santa Claus tomorrow.

Little Joe stood outside the ten-cent store in the light, and the snow, and people passing. Gee, Christmas was pretty. All tinsel and stars and cotton. And Santa Claus a-coming from somewhere, dropping things in stockings. And all the people in the streets were carrying things, and the kids looked happy.

But Joe soon got tired of just standing and thinking and waiting in front of the ten-cent store. There were so many things to look at in the other windows. He moved along up the block a little, and then a little more, walking and looking. In fact, he moved until he came to the white folks' picture show.

In the lobby of the moving picture show, behind the plate glass doors, it was all warm and glowing and awful pretty. Joe stood looking in, and as he looked his eyes began to make out, in there blazing beneath holly and colored streamers and the electric stars of the lobby, a marvelous Christmas tree. A group of children and grown-ups, white, of course, were standing around a big jovial man in red beside the tree. Or was it a man? Little Joe's eyes opened wide. No, it was not a man at all. It was Santa Claus!

Little Joe pushed open one of the glass doors and ran into the lobby of the white moving picture show. Little Joe went right through the crowd and up to where he could get a good look at Santa Claus. And Santa Claus was giving away gifts, little presents for children, little boxes of animal crackers and stick-candy canes. And behind him on the tree was a big sign (which little Joe didn't know how to read). It said, to those who understood, MERRY XMAS FROM SANTA CLAUS TO OUR YOUNG PATRONS.

Around the lobby, other signs said, WHEN YOU COME OUT OF THE SHOW STOP WITH YOUR CHILDREN AND SEE OUR SANTA CLAUS. And another announced, GEM THEATRE MAKES ITS CUSTOMERS HAPPY—SEE OUR SANTA.

And there was Santa Claus in a red suit and a white beard all sprinkled with tinsel snow. Around him were rattles and drums and rocking horses which he was not giving away. But the signs on them said (could little Joe have read) that they would be presented from the stage on Christmas Day to the holders of lucky numbers. Tonight, Santa Claus was only giving away candy, and stick-candy canes, and animal crackers to the kids.

Joe would have liked terribly to have a stick-candy cane. He came a little closer to Santa Claus, until he was right in front of the crowd. And then Santa Claus saw Joe.

Why is it that lots of white people always grin when they see a Negro child? Santa Claus grinned. Everybody else grinned, too, looking at little black Joe—who had no business in the lobby of a white theatre. Then Santa Claus stooped down and slyly picked up one of his lucky number rattles, a great big loud tin-pan rattle such as they use in cabarets. And he shook it fiercely right at Joe. That was funny. The white people laughed, kids and all. But little Joe didn't laugh. He was scared. To the shaking of the big rattle, he turned and fled out of the warm lobby of the theatre, out into the street where the snow was and the people. Frightened by laughter, he had begun to cry. He went looking for his mama. In his heart he never thought Santa Claus shook great rattles at children like that—and then laughed.

In the crowd on the street he went the wrong way. He couldn't find the ten-cent store or his mother. There were too many people, all white people, moving like white shadows in the snow, a world of white people.

It seemed to Joe an awfully long time till he suddenly saw Arcie, dark and worried-looking, cut across the side-walk through the passing crowd and grab him. Although her arms were full of packages, she still managed with one free hand to shake him until his teeth rattled.

"Why didn't you stand where I left you?" Arcie demanded loudly. "Tired as I am, I got to run all over the streets in the night lookin' for you. I'm a great mind to wear you out."

When little Joe got his breath back, on the way home, he told his mama he had been in the moving picture show.

"But Santa Claus didn't give me nothin'," Joe said tearfully. "He made a big noise at me and I runned out."

"Serves you right," said Arcie, trudging through the snow. "You had no business in there. I told you to stay where I left you."

"But I seed Santa Claus in there," little Joe said, "so I went in."

"Huh! That wasn't no Santa Claus," Arcie explained. "If it was, he wouldn't a-treated you like that. That's a theatre for white folks—I told you once—and he's just a old white man."

"Oh . . . ," said little Joe.

Commie Christmas

Wendell Mayo

Bunk aloft, I kicked off my bedspread embroidered with a Redstone rocket racing toward a deep blue quadrant of space. I swung past the safety rail and gazed down, through clearing mists of sleep, to see Allen's bunk, bunker really, where he cowered from unseen foes, in fetal coil, thumb in mouth, unnatural at the age of six.

"Get your thumb out your mouth," I said, feeling like that thumb, Christmas vacation, 1962, sucked into a shriveled existence as his older brother, bunkmate, sharing everything.

Allen's thumb popped out, revealed buck teeth, the result of constant vectors of thumb-force tugging outward. His eyes swam and opened, unperturbed by Mom's slamming the dryer door and Dad's hammering in the half-basement before going to work, his project to relocate me to that darker region of the house, where the furnace growled hourly into flame and breathed life into our Cleveland split-level.

"What do Santie's reindeer eat, anyway?" Allen asked.

Santie was the diminutive term Dad had used growing up, though he stopped using it after he got his job at NASA's Lewis Research Center, some top secret project. But Allen picked up the word. Only weeks after the Cuban Missile Crisis ended, and Allen went on and on about Santie, as if the world had never been on the brink of annihilation. I wouldn't have known about the Missile Crisis, only Dad had set up the old Westinghouse in the half-basement and I snuck down to watch coverage of the blockade.

The TV sputtered—

mostly sunny and cold
Cuban missile crisis expected to have little effect
  on the cost of living
talks take on a graver aspect
full retaliatory response possible
flurries ending later this evening

"Reindeer eat Atomic apples," I informed Allen.

"Will we find reindeer shit in the snow?"

"Only if you step in it."

"But what will it look like?"

"Glowing," I said, hooked my toes in the spindles of the footboard of my bunk, swooped in lower, hovered over him. "Just shut up about reindeers. Santie's a Commie, anyway."

"Is not!" His words shot straight past a suspicious fragment of dried oatmeal cloying in a corner of his mouth. I doubted Allen even knew what a Commie was, only that it had to be bad, but I didn't care. I made such ugly accusations—even about someone like Santie—and a part of me knew they weren't true. But then I wondered: If I could think Santie was a Commie, then it could be true; otherwise I wouldn't have thought it in the first place. And if Santie was a Commie, then it explained why he never brought me the one thing I wanted above all, the one luxurious thing no self-respecting Commie would ever ask for, a Nine Transistor Realtone Radio, because if he got it he'd be sent to a gulag. No other kid I knew had a transistor radio, let alone a Nine Transistor. So I pinned my hopes for the Nine Transistor not on Santie, but on the Missile Crisis itself. I imagined Dad and Mom embracing, relieved we'd not be bombed into nonexistence, clutching one another, teary eyed, Dad saying, "Maybe, just this once, we ought to get Bud that Nine Transistor Realtone he's been wanting," and Mom blubbering, "Get him anything he wants, anything, no matter how expensive—in case we're blown to bits!"

Allen's translucent thumb rocketed into his mouth, then popped right out.

"If Santie's a Commie," he said, "then how come he brings toys to kids?"

"That's exactly why he is a Commie. Santie wants to take all the toys and spread them around to everyone, same as what Commies want to do with everyone's money."

"So what's wrong with that?"

I rolled a little over the sideboard so I could make eye contact with him. I wanted him to remember this, big brother to little brother, my eyes dead on his, locked tight like the latest missile guidance system I imagined Dad worked on at NASA.

"You know those redheaded, cross-eyed Healy brothers that live next to Regina Mountcastle's? You remember how they chased me down with their big red Schwinns last summer? How thcy ran me and my new bike clean into the ditch? How I told Dad I'd done it myself because if I said Healy brothers did it he'd ask me to go after them?

A sucking sound, and the thumb went in. I could hear him working the big digit against his front teeth.

"Do you really think Healy brothers deserve the same as you and me for Christmas? Do you think they deserve the same money and stuff as us? Not everyone deserves the same as everyone else. Especially Healy brothers."

Since we were on the subject of sharing, I leapt down to Allen's bunk and snatched the steel Tonka truck out his bed things. That Tonka had been mine before Dad gave it to Allen, saying, "Share and share alike, Bud." I shot up, regained my bunk, but not before he took hold of the Tonka. I clamped my toes onto the spindles of the footboard.

"Gimme that truck, you little Commie," I said.

I hauled up on the Tonka, he hauled down, until I had him moving back and forth, let him think we were in a stalemate of awesome forces—then I let go.

After I conked Allen with the Tonka, Mom confined me to our room while Allen paraded about the house, a flesh-colored band-aid affixed to his upper lip like a comical dictator's moustache. But I knew Mom would let me out soon. She couldn't resist the Snow Road Cinema, and it wasn't long before she backed the Fairlane out the garage, ordered us into the car, stuck her *Yellow Pages* to the driver's seat, boosted herself on it, and took off for the Snow Road. Once inside the dark, projector-lit theater, a thin, wicked little smile jetted across her face. When the feature started, *Invasion of the Body Snatchers,* she whispered, "Do NOT tell your dad," and we wagged our heads emphatically in the affirmative. She knew that Dad, our brilliant scientist, had forbidden any of us to have first contact with invaders in film, television, and any form that such invaders might take. "Those movies aren't true," Dad had warned us. Once, I asked him the truth about outer space, what he worked on at NASA. He wrinkled his brow, took his thick, black, horn-rims off, and licked both lenses. "I can't tell you, boy," he said . solemnly, then snuck a handkerchief out his hip pocket and wiped the lenses dry. I wondered if the CIA had programmed his lens-licking response. Say an enemy agent asked him about top secret matters. He'd automatically lick his lenses and that would remind him to clam up. Once, just after the Missile Crisis, I told him I wanted the Nine Transistor for Christmas. "We'll see," he said and licked his lenses, obviously hiding something big.

Soon, Mom, Allen and I found ourselves surrounded by slimy pods developing into copies of real people—then disposing of the originals. It happened while the real people slept. When I glanced over at Allen, he slumped sideways in his seat, thumb planted in the frothy soil of his mouth. I shook him awake.

"Hey," I whispered one of those raspy whispers, so loud you may as well have not whispered. "You wanna become an alien or something?" Of course, I knew Allen wasn't an alien; it just came out my mouth—and because of that it seemed true. The Allen that sat next to me might be a copy of the original kid, perhaps some pact Commies had with aliens to duplicate Americans and infiltrate the country, which was why Allen hadn't stopped sucking his thumb when normal kids had.

When we returned from the Snow Road, Mom surprised me by ordering my continued incarceration in our bedroom for lacerating Allen's lip. After serving another half-hour, Allen—Pod Kid—came to visit me. I toed a spindle at the footboard of my bunk until it squeaked a little, a sign Allen usually got, one that meant leave me alone. But he jacked up on tiptoes and poked me in a rib with his wet thumb.

"At least Santie's elves ain't Commies," he said.

"They're worst of all!" I said. "They slave for Santie in his toy-shop. What if they want to be more than toy makers? You think they have a choice?"

"Mom's putting the new tree up. You coming?"

"Do I have a choice?"

I rolled on my side, squinted at him, thinking if I squinted tightly my eyelashes might polarize light just enough to allow me to see Allen's true Commie-alien self, O-mouthed and ready to point and squeal at anyone different from him. Then Mom called us, so I followed Allen into the hallway.

Outside bedrooms on the second level, you could see the entire living and dining rooms at one stretch. I loved to gaze out over the vast unclaimed space, exist just a little above everything, have it all to myself—except for Santie, that is. His plastic figure sat on the dining room hutch, Buddha-style, laughing behind a Cossack moustache, conspiratorial wink, and Coca-Cola pressed to his jolly red lips. How could such a strange creature be described as anything but Commie? Allen passed Commie Claus several times a day, thoughtlessly squeaking, "Hi, Santie!" And just when I thought Santie was the only other claimant to my space, in a far corner of the living room I spotted our new Gleam-All aluminum Christmas tree, with pom-pom branches and special twist needles. Near the base of the metal tree, the electric color wheel ground away, soaking the tree's reflective branches deep red; then yellow, blazing like a solar flare; then deep blue, like a cold, icy inward glare; and finally green, fresh lawn-cut green, reminding me how much I hated winter.

Mom went to her bedroom to fetch a box of trimmings. Pod-boy fell to his knees, galloped on all fours toward the tree, then stood in a trance before the metallic chameleon, until I worried that the Sputnik tree topper might be sending Commie instructions out through the limbs and into his impressionable mind.

I grabbed his shoulders. "Snap out of it," I said and shook him hard. "That tree isn't normal. It's a Commie tree."

"It's . . . not." One side of his face glowed blue and he seemed puzzled, as if I'd reached some small cluster of normal brain cells in my so-called brother's head.

⋅⋅⋅

After Dad got home from NASA, Mom found me in the half-finished basement, announced, "We're going for ice cream." When I didn't reply, she hesitated, just the way I liked her to. "Stay if you like," she added. "We won't be long." Her eyes darted to the cinderblock wall behind my bed, beyond which the Molloys's driveway and house lay. "Call Molloys if you need anything."

She closed the basement door and I heard a rubbery commotion, the three of them suiting up, and Mom's warnings: Allen this, Allen that, Pod Kid silent as ever, then the moment I longed for—they left and I reached for the paperback on my bed, Dickens's *A Christmas Carol*. Cheap, but I liked how the pebbled faux leather surface felt in my hands, the scent of new ink when I stuck my nose to its inner spine. I belonged there, in my cinderblock quarters, buried in snow, no way out except in pages of a novel, eyes devouring word after word as Ebenezer first hears Marley's ghost wail, his clamorous chains on wooden stairs, ascending, higher, closer, all while my spine numbed against the stone wall. After a time, I heard a second chorus of clanking chains seeming to come from outside our house! I read on—hearing Marley's shackles rat-

56

tling in and out my head, mixed with moaning snowbound wind. I pressed an ear to a cinderblock. The sound was unmistakable. Horrors! Chains! I threw the book aside, crossed the cold clay tiles to the window, saw white flakes, rankled and riotous, careen into uneven walls and soft mounds of snow-covered building materials for new houses under construction, most dark inside, un-sided, open to elements, where streetlamp light glinted off aluminum backing and insulation. But no real source of Marley's lamentation. Was this to be my fate in the wake of the Missile Crisis? Hallucination? Madness? I heard our back door open, Dad's Corvair puttering, Allen stomp upstairs, run water in the sink. Then I heard Dad and Mom come in.

"Snow's getting deep out there," Dad told Mom. "I saw Molloy next door putting chains on his tires. Guess I better get ours on pretty soon."

When Mom came to send me upstairs to bed, I pretended to be asleep, a tactic that got me a whole night in the unfinished basement to ponder the miracle of Marley's chains. Next morning was Christmas Eve and snow had stopped falling. From my half-finished basement window I saw brilliant light glance off the same new construction—speckled roofing shingles, insulation and backing mirrored and shining, the name ARMSTRONG flickering under a flawless blue winter sky, the half-finished homes looking nothing like they had the night before, their hypnotic allure under streetlamp-lit flying snow. I realized that the miracle of Marley's chains was just that—a miracle that I came to see there were no miracles—a miracle that I realized imagined things had real world counterparts, that they clung to one another, unbreakable as Molloy's tire chains.

Allen shuffled in.

"Maybe Santie's not a Commie," I grumbled.

"He's not?"

"Yeah—because he doesn't exist."

"Does to!"

"Santie's not a Commie—but you are."

"I ain't no Commie," Allen said, and shish-shushed his way over my clay tiles at remarkable speed, heading for the door. I knew Allen wasn't a Commie. But I was angry at him for his inexplicable faith in Santie to fulfill his Christmas dreams, while I depended on the A-bomb to create the bottomless terror Mom and Dad may have felt in the Missile Crisis and its psychological after-effects, which I could only hope included their splurging on my Nine Transistor.

I pursued Allen upstairs.

"I can tell if you're a Commie," I said, snagged his unoccupied hand, yanked him down the hallway, and shoved him into the bathroom. I tapped the door shut, locked it, pointed to the sink. "Put your head in there." I seized him by the shoulders, forced his noggin down, freed one hand, ran water, snagged a bar of Ivory soap, and dragged it across the stiff hairs on the back of his neck. "Don't move," I whispered, took Dad's twin-blade razor in hand, swiped it across his neck, and removed a horizontal patch of hair. "I'm looking for the scar where Commies implanted your brain control device."

"I'm telling Mom," he whimpered, rubbed the back of his neck, started crying, unsnapped the lock, ran out, and called, "Mom! Mom!" until I heard him find her in the distant recesses of the split-level, then the crescendo as she clomped her way toward me and appeared in the doorframe of the bathroom.

"Are you crazy?" she asked, but I didn't answer. I kept looking at her holiday apron, the flour-dusted image of Commie Claus, winking at me!

Christmas morning, Mom and Dad shish-shushed into the living room, sat on the sofa, eyes half-closed, heads together in the shape of a teepee, until Dad realized the color wheel was stuck on red, snapped up, nearly toppling Mom, and slapped the wheel into motion—yellow, blue, green, fiery red again. Seeing such a sign of life from Dad, Allen propelled himself with both arms across the ocean of carpet, knees digging deeper into the pile, until he reached the angular mound of presents at the base of the Gleam-All tree. He tore away at them, and when he found a box obviously mine kicked it aside and ravaged another. I picked up his leavings, first one from Santie, a pair of manmade neoprene oxfords, space-age pedestrian technology; then an Atomic Cape Canaveral Missile Base Set, a leviathan of a box I could scarcely grasp with both arms at full extension, its contents rattling, shifting side to side, and me with it, like a sailor on deck in a stormy sea. Last, amidst the utter ruin of our living room, I discovered an old Marlboro carton—Dad's smokes?—but the tag read, FROM MOM AND DAD WITH LOVE. I shot them both a look, and when they smiled from within their teepee, I knew I had them—they had a habit of disguising their best gifts in ordinary boxes. I was so sure it was my Nine Transistor that I took my time popping the lid, all the while congratulating myself for correctly psycho-analyzing my parents in the wake of the Missile Crisis. I slid the weighty device into my eager hands—a block of wood, a tuning coil, resistor with many-colored bands, a diode, stuff I'd seen in Dad's mason jar of electrical odd and ends, all soldered together with brightly coated wire—red, blue, yellow, green—oh! that metal tree! Then out the Marlboro box slid a large alligator clip and one of Dad's black bakelite Navy headphones. I looked at Dad and Mom, saw their eyes shining out their teepee.

"What is it?" I asked them, half my mouth smiling for Mom, the other crinkled in confusion for Dad.

"A radio," Dad said.

"He made it himself, Bud," Mom added.

I studied the circuitry, they unstuck their teepee heads.

"How many transistors?" I asked.

"Doesn't need them," he replied. "No batteries, either. It's a miracle radio!"

A short while I watched Allen play with toys like other kids got, a Superman tray puzzle, Lincoln Logs, a gyroscope. When he set the gyroscope atop the puzzle box and yanked the cord it jumped out his hands and leapt onto Mom's toes. Dad repacked his cigarettes into the Marlboro carton and, as he instructed, I took the miracle radio to the half-basement and into the crawlspace. There I ventured, knees and hands, holding my flashlight, its beam jittering over old spider webs draping joists, rusted nail ends, and pale-green cinderblocks. When I reached the water lines, splotched white and turquoise, I stuck the flashlight between my knees and clamped the alligator clip to the water main. I pressed the old Navy headphone to my ear, turned the tuner slowly, and listened the way the last kid on Earth might listen for some sign of life in nuclear winter—and in that moment I felt something give. If I was the only kid alive on earth, then I could do anything. I waited to feel guilty about being the only kid alive, but I didn't. Not even the power of the A-bomb had instilled enough guilt in my parents to provide me with my dying wish, my Nine Transistor, so why should I feel guilty? No sound came from the miracle radio, and when I returned upstairs to the scene of devastation under the base of the Gleam-All tree, shredded wrapping and ribbons in Möbius strips of confounding coils about Allen's knees and shoulders, Dad asked, "You pick up anything?"

"Yeah," I said. "It's just really hard to make out."

I seized my Atomic Cape Canaveral Missile Base box, tore the tag off, FROM SANTIE—my foot!—poured its contents onto the carpet near the Gleam-All, and invested hours setting it up, ignoring the instructions, the maddening color wheel war-painting my face red, yellow, green, blue, guided only by the feeling of freedom I'd gotten in the crawlspace. Each piece snapped into place: the Missile Research Center, gantry, various launchers, a rouges gallery of rockets, drawn straight from mythology—Thor, Atlas, Jupiter, Titan—and one other, Redstone—the rock in my David's sling. From across the vast expanse of the living room, I eyed my Goliath, the grinning Commie Claus, so satisfied by my failure in my quest for the Nine Transistor. I took the Redstone in hand, removed the Mercury capsule and replaced it with a hard-rubber nuclear warhead. I set the missile on my biggest launcher, a blue job with an eight-inch spring, and pulled it back into position, while each inch the tempered steel creaked against the plastic launch lug. When the missile clicked into place, I consulted the compass and set it due North—the Pole, of course!—then carefully adjusted the firing angle so the weapon would fly clear across the living room, dining room, to the hutch, then strike Commie Claus right between his laughing eyes. Maybe, just maybe by firing the missile across such vast, unclaimed space, by obliterating the symbol of my defeat, I thought I might claim one thing for myself, one impossible posthumous shot. I fingered the firing lever—when Allen furrowed his way to me, rolled onto his back, shrieked, "No, not Santie!" reached in, and deflected my missile into the curtains.

<hr />

Less than a year later Kennedy passed and two after that Vietnam escalated, about the time Dad went with the Gemini Space Project. Allen and I were separated, got our own rooms, mine in the finished half-basement. Early January, 1966, Dad fired up the Corvair and for the first time drove us to the Brook Park Police Station, near the tennis courts and City Pool, lit only by a distant streetlamp. There, people piled their dead trees high as our split-level, then circled the heap under a new moon and starless sky. Allen stood beside me, hands stuffed deep in the pockets of his peacoat, a habit he'd developed in the process of learning what to with his wayward thumb. I remember a caravan of black dogs passed us, three pink tongues behind a panting fog, driven by a man in a long green coat, who glanced at me from beneath his broad hood. I whispered "Wait," then thought, Marley!—and wondered how he'd found the power to free himself of his chains. When a cop ignited the pile of trees, a fat woman wearing a hat like a Cossack's papakha shouted "Jesus lights the world!" and the pile burst, showered white sparks on people, shot ghost-gray smoke above, forced me back with others, while Allen remained at the very edge of the inferno, removed his hand from a pocket, and chewed on his glistening paw until Mom leapt in and hurried him back to safety.

Allen shivered once and asked me, "Santie doesn't really exist, does he?"

"Sure he does," I replied. "He was a Commie. I tried to wipe him out with a nuclear warhead. You saved him, remember?"

The snapping fire cooled to orange and people inched toward it, laughing, sharing stories of how they'd survived the massive explosion.

Allen smiled, said, "Did you really think Santie was a Commie?"

I watched Mom and Dad, waiting for us by the tattered nets of summer and empty City Pool encrusted with old clay-brown ice. Coals of the exhausted fire glowed so red they seemed blood, so bloody they made the starless sky seem darker.

"I don't know," I said, and he stuffed his hand securely into his pocket. "Just do me a favor. Next time I try to nuke Santie, you save him again, okay?" Then Allen started laughing like the others, the way you laugh when you know you should be shock-silent. "Allen," I groaned, "please!"

Ohio Waiting for Camels

Rane Arroyo

Christmas was once a family affair: relatives showing up with relatives showing up with relatives whose names were vagaries linked by DNA. Excess was a demand, a normalcy, until my puberty and I had to love men. Things changed when I was no longer welcomed as a gay man, as a Latino who betrayed lineage and laterality.

Eventually, after many mistakes, after many wrong Christmases, I fell in love. Soon, I inherited my mother when Papi returned to Puerto Rico to die among strangers. It was and continues to be an adjustment. My partner has a mother-in-law even if the law part isn't actualized yet.

We decided to have a Christmas party of three: the us in USA. Mami didn't really want to come but not because of my partner. She loves him. I understood though: the absence. Who wouldn't be there with us—the dead, the far away, the past. She was embarrassed by the abundance we shared with her since it's like a book one reads aloud and enjoys.

We were in Toledo, Ohio, a city I never heard of but somehow is now home. I think of Mami looking out of the windows and saying, "It's hard to think about how one sky goes over the world." Nothing pretentious. No wonder that I became a poet.

We decided on a "real" tree this year and Mami talked about artificial trees, how they don't shed, no need to water them, how shiny the fake branches are in a dark world. My partner laughed, "You and your mother are so much alike."

It wasn't a perfect Christmas: not like in *The Waltons,* the end of *It's a Wonderful Life.* Three souls in a simple living room living despite the odds against us early on. Mami could afford to buy us each a coffee cup, a treasure beyond cost. I knew she was sad that my brother and sister were strewn across the continent, that cousins and family somehow were skewed in the Republican era of me first.

"Mami," I said, "Do you remember the camels?"

"Ah," she replied in her neutral voice, "You were too young to remember. You remember what I told you."

My partner, by then, was used to the rip tides rhetoric.

He sat and watched us, gave me a wink.

"I remember."

"You're too young to remember things."

It's like a compliment and a chagrin at the same time.

"I waited for those camels."

Three Kings' Day. We used to leave grass for the camels. Forget the kings, but the camels, in Chicago, that was exciting.

"Maybe they'll find us in Ohio."

"Maybe."

The three of us eat, pose for pictures that reveal little about ourselves.

How did my mother end up living with me and my gay partner after Papi declared me dead—even to his deathbed? I had stopped existing.

But not on Christmas or other holidays.

My brother and sister called, nephews and nieces talking about the prize in being alive on that day.

My mother's birthday is on Christmas.

Act of God, if one believes in significance.

Practical gifts, including bags of peanuts, for Mami's backyard squirrels.

What stands out though is that it felt normal.

Mami, my boyfriend, the family traditions—all there, in our Ohio. Ours by the power of presence.

Mami walked to the tree and smelled it: "It's a good green."

A small moment that perhaps she doesn't even remember, but for me offers a powerful image. The tree cut and transplanted into our living room for weeks became a teacher about rootlessness being the danger. Mami didn't stay long; there were phone calls to her awaiting her voice. How I wanted someone with perhaps over-emotional reactions to things, but I've surrounded myself with those who feel deeply and say what they must. I'm one stupid guy who would sit on Santa's lap no matter my age, but I'm too adult even for myself.

And Santa might be a cute guy behind the masquerade of kindness. Or worse, he might define kindness. Yes, I like soap operas.

We dropped Mami off at the house we bought her.

She said, "Ohio, who would have imagined?"

I thought: one, her English is superior; two, she's going to be depressed so tomorrow I'll do my best to convince her that French toast is like medicine; three, she is not alone since she has us.

A quiet Christmas, done by five p.m. Mami likes things early the older she gets.

My boyfriend and I kiss and also let go of the tense day. Making other people happy can be hard labor.

I remember that Christmas with my boyfriend driving, my mother feeling like she belonged somewhere, and me turning on the radio. Ohio was everywhere. I was in Ohio. Me. It wasn't the time with X in the Rockies or with another X in California. This was my real life now and how real I felt.

I tried to be my boyfriend's best gift ever.

Those camels were wiser than the wise men. They bore the burdens and then just ate, renewed themselves. Christmas is about renewal. Imaginary or not, they fed me as I fed them as a young and lost boy in an America still growing up. Grass for them which is the color of go, go.

Christmas; or, The Good Fairy

Harriet Beecher Stowe

"Oh, dear! Christmas is coming in a fortnight, and I have got to think up presents for everybody!" said young Ellen Stuart, as she leaned languidly back in her chair. "Dear me, it's so tedious! Everybody has got everything that can be thought of."

"Oh, no," said her confidential adviser, Miss Lester, in a soothing tone. "You have means of buying everything you can fancy; and when every shop and store is glittering with all number of splendors, you cannot surely be at a loss."

"Well, now, just listen. To begin with, there's mamma. What can I get for her? I have thought of ever so many things. She has three card cases, four gold thimbles, two or three gold chains, two writing desks of different patterns; and then as to rings, broaches, boxes, and all other things, I should think she might be sick of the sight of them. I am sure I am," said she, languidly gazing on her white and jeweled fingers.

This view of the case seemed rather puzzling to the adviser, and there was silence for a few minutes, when Ellen, yawning, resumed:—

"And then there's cousins Jane and Mary; I suppose they will be coming down on me with a whole load of presents; and Mrs. B. will send me something—she did last year; and then there's cousins William and Tom—I must get them something; and I would like to do it well enough, if I only knew what to get."

"Well," said Eleanor's aunt, who had been sitting quietly rattling her knitting needles during this speech, "it's a pity that you had not such a subject to practice on as I when I was a girl. Presents did not fly about in those days as they do now. I remember, when I was ten years old, my father gave me a most marvelously ugly sugar dog for a Christmas gift, and I was perfectly delighted with it, the very idea of a present was so new to us."

"Dear aunt, how delighted I should be if I had any such fresh, unsophisticated body to get presents for! But to get and get for people that have more than they know what to do with now; to add pictures, books, and gilding when the centre tables are loaded with them now, and rings and jewels when they are a perfect drug! I wish myself that I were not sick, and sated and tired with having everything in the world given me."

"Well, Eleanor," said her aunt, "if you really do want unsophisticated subjects to practice on, I can put you in the way of it. I can show you more than one family to whom you might seem to be a very good fairy, and where such gifts as you could give with all ease would seem like a magic dream."

"Why, that would really be worth while, aunt."

"Look over in that back alley," said her aunt. "You see those buildings?"

"That miserable row of shanties? Yes."

"Well, I have several acquaintances there who have never been tired of Christmas gifts or gifts of any other kind. I assure you, you could make quite a sensation over there."

"Well, who is there? Let us know."

"Do you remember Owen, that used to make your shoes?"

"Yes, I remember something about him."

"Well, he has fallen into a consumption, and cannot work any more; and he, and his wife, and three little children live in one of the rooms."

"How do they get along?"

"His wife takes in sewing sometimes, and sometimes goes out washing. Poor Owen! I was over there yesterday; he looks thin and wasted, and his wife was saying that he was parched with constant fever, and had very little appetite. She had, with great self-denial, and by restricting herself almost of necessary food, got him two or three oranges; and the poor fellow seemed so eager after them."

"Poor fellow!" said Eleanor, involuntarily.

"Now," said her aunt, "suppose Owen's wife should get up on Christmas morning and find at the door a couple of dozen of oranges, and some nice white grapes, such as you had at your party last week; don't you think it would make a sensation?"

"Why, yes, I think very likely it might; but who else, aunt? You spoke of a great many."

"Well, on the lower floor there is a neat little room, that is always kept perfectly trim and tidy; it belongs to a young couple who have nothing beyond the husband's day wages to live on. They are, nevertheless, as cheerful and chipper as a couple of wrens; and she is up and down half a dozen times a day, to help poor Mrs. Owen. She has a baby of her own about five months old, and of course does all the cooking, washing, and ironing for herself and husband; and yet, when Mrs. Owen goes out to wash, she takes her baby, and keeps it whole days for her."

"I'm sure she deserves that the good fairies should smile on her," said Eleanor; "one baby exhausts my stock of virtues very rapidly."

"But you ought to see her baby," said Aunt E.; "so plump, so rosy, and good-natured, and always clean as a lily. This baby is a sort of household shrine; nothing is too sacred or too good for it; and I believe the little thrifty woman feels only one temptation to be extravagant, and that is to get some ornaments to adorn this little divinity."

"Why, did she ever tell you so?"

"No; but one day, when I was coming down stairs, the door of their room was partly open, and I saw a peddler there with open box. John, the husband, was standing with a little purple cap on his hand, which he was regarding with a mystified, admiring air, as if he didn't quite comprehend it, and trim little Mary gazing at it with longing eyes.

"'I think we might get it,' said John."

"'Oh, no,' said she, regretfully; 'yet I wish we could, it's so pretty!'"

"Say no more, aunt. I see the good fairy must pop a cap into the window on Christmas morning. Indeed, it shall be done. How they will wonder where it came from, and talk about it for months to come!"

"Well, then," continued her aunt, "in the next street to ours there is a miserable building, that looks as if it were just going to topple over; and away up in the third story, in a little room just under the eaves, live two poor, lonely old women. They are both nearly on to ninety. I was in there day before yesterday. One of them is constantly confined to her bed with rheumatism; the other, weak and feeble, with failing sight and trembling hands, totters about, her only helper; and they are entirely dependent on charity."

"Can't they do anything? Can't they knit?" said Eleanor.

"You are young and strong, Eleanor, and have quick eyes and nimble fingers; how long would it take you to knit a pair of stockings?"

"I?" said Eleanor. "What an idea! I never tried, but I think I could get a pair done in a week, perhaps."

"And if somebody gave you twenty-five cents for them, and out of this you had to get food, and pay room rent, and buy coal for your fire, and oil for your lamp—"

"Stop, aunt, for pity's sake!"

"Well, I will stop; but they can't; they must pay so much every month for that miserable shell they live in, or be turned into the street. The meal and flour that some kind person sends goes off for them just as it does for others, and they must get more or starve; and coal is now scarce and high priced."

"O aunt, I'm quite convinced, I'm sure; don't run me down and annihilate me with all these terrible realities. What shall I do to play good fairy to these old women?"

"If you will give me full power, Eleanor, I will put up a basket to be sent to them that will give them something to remember all winter."

"Oh, certainly I will. Let me see if I can't think of something myself."

"Well, Eleanor, suppose, then, some fifty or sixty years hence, if you were old, and your father, and mother, and aunts, and uncles, now so thick around you, lay cold and silent in so many graves—you have somehow got away off to a strange city, where you were never known—you live in a miserable garret, where snow blows at night through the cracks, and the fire is very apt to go out in the old cracked stove—you sit crouching over the dying embers that evening before Christmas—nobody to speak to you, nobody to care for you, except another poor old soul who lies moaning in the bed. Now, what would you like to have sent to you?"

"O aunt, what a dismal picture!"

"And yet, Ella, all poor, forsaken old women are made of young girls, who expected it in their youth as little as you do, perhaps."

"Say no more, aunt. I'll buy—let me see—a comfortable warm shawl for each of these poor women; and I'll send them—let me see—oh, some tea—nothing goes down with old women like tea; and I'll make John wheel some coal over to them; and, aunt, it would not be a very bad thought to send them a new stove. I remember, the other day, when mamma was pricing stoves, I saw some such nice ones for two or three dollars."

"For a new hand, Ella, you work up the idea very well," said her aunt.

"But how much ought I to give, for any one case, to these women, say?"

"How much did you give last year for any single Christmas present?"

"Why, six or seven dollars for some; those elegant souvenirs were seven dollars; that ring I gave Mrs. B. was twenty."

"And do you suppose Mrs. B. was any happier for it?"

"No, really, I don't think she cared much about it; but I had to give her something, because she had sent me something the year before, and I did not want to send a paltry present to one in her circumstances."

"Then, Ella, give the same to any poor, distressed, suffering creature who really needs it, and see in how many forms of good such a sum will appear. That one hard, cold, glittering ring, that now cheers nobody, and means nothing, that you give because you must, and she takes because she must, might, if broken up into smaller sums, send real warm and heartfelt gladness through many a cold and cheerless dwelling, through many an aching heart."

"You are getting to be an orator, aunt; but don't you approve of Christmas presents, among friends and equals?"

"Yes, indeed," said her aunt, fondly stroking her head. "I have had some Christmas presents that did me a world of good—a little book mark, for instance, that a certain niece of mine worked for me, with wonderful secrecy, three years ago, when she was a young lady with a purse full of money—that book mark was a true Christmas present; and my young people across the way are plotting a profound surprise to each other on Christmas morning. John has contrived, by an hour of extra work every night, to lay by enough to get Mary a new calico dress; and she, poor soul, has bargained away the only thing in the jewelry line she ever possessed, to be laid out on a new hat for him.

"I know, too, a washerwoman who has a poor lame boy—a patient, gentle little fellow—who has lain quietly for weeks and months in his little crib, and his mother is going to give him a splendid Christmas present."

"What is it, pray?"

"A whole orange! Don't laugh. She will pay ten whole cents for it; for it shall be none of your common oranges, but a picked one of the very best going! She has put by the money, a cent at a time, for a whole month; and nobody knows which will be happiest in it, Willie or his mother. These are such Christmas presents as I like to think of—gifts coming from love, and tending to produce love; these are the appropriate gifts of the day."

"But don't you think that it's right for those who *have* money to give expensive presents, supposing always, as you say, they are given from real affection?"

"Sometimes, undoubtedly. The Saviour did not condemn her who broke an alabaster box of ointment—very precious—simply as a proof of love, although the suggestion was made, 'This might have been sold for three hundred pence, and given to the poor.' I have thought he would regard with sympathy the fond efforts which human love sometimes makes to express itself by gifts, the rarest and most costly. How I rejoiced with all my heart, when Charles Elton gave his poor mother that splendid Chinese shawl and gold watch! Because I knew they came from the very fullness of his heart to a mother that he could not do too much for—a mother that has done and suffered everything for him. In some such cases, when resources are ample, a costly gift seems to have a graceful appropriateness; but I cannot approve of it if it exhausts all the means of doing for the poor; it is better, then, to give a simple offering, and to do something for those who really need it."

Eleanor looked thoughtful; her aunt laid down her knitting, and said, in a tone of gentle seriousness, "Whose birth does Christmas commemorate, Ella?"

"Our Saviour's, certainly, aunt."

"Yes," said her aunt. "And when and how was he born? In a stable! Laid in a manger; thus born, that in all ages he might be known as the brother and friend of the poor, the outcast, and distressed; and if Christ should come back to our city on a Christmas day, where should we think it most appropriate to his character to find him? Would he be carrying splendid gifts to splendid dwellings, desolate, the poor, the forsaken, and the sorrowful?"

And here the conversation ended.

"What sort of Christmas presents is Ella buying?" said Cousin Tom, as the waiter handed in a portentous-looking package, which had been just rung in at the door.

"Let's open it," said saucy Will. "Upon my word, two great gray blanket shawls! These must be for you and me, Tom! And what's this? A great bolt of cotton flannel and gray yarn stockings!"

The door bell rang again, and the waiter brought in another bulky parcel, and deposited it on the marble-topped centre table.

"What's here?" said Will, cutting the cord. "Whew! A perfect nest of packages! Oolong tea! Oranges! Grapes! White sugar! Bless me, Ella must be going to homekeeping!"

"Or going crazy!" said Tom; "and on my word," said he, looking out of the window, "there's a drayman ringing at our door, with a stove, with a teakettle set in the top of it!"

"Ella's cook stove, of course," said Will; and just at this moment the young lady entered, with her purse hanging gracefully over her hand.

"Now, boys, you are too bad!" she exclaimed, as each of the mischievous youngsters was gravely marching up and down, attired in a gray shawl.

"Didn't you get them for us? We thought you did," said both.

"Ella, I want some of that cotton flannel, to make me a pair of pantaloons," said Tom.

"I say, Ella," said Will, "when are you going to housekeeping? Your cooking stove is standing down in the street; 'pon my word, John is loading some coal on the dray with it."

"Ella, isn't that going to be sent to my office?" said Tom; "do you know I do so languish for a new stove with a teakettle in the top, to heat a fellow's shaving water!"

Just then, another ring at the door, and the grinning waiter handed in a small brown paper parcel for Miss Ella. Tom made a dive at it, and staying off the brown paper, developed a jaunty little purple velvet cap, with silver tassels.

"My smoking cap, as I live!" said he; "only I shall have to wear it on my thumb, instead of my head—too small entirely," said he, shaking his head gravely.

"Come, you saucy boys," said Aunt E., entering briskly, "what are you teasing Ella for?"

"Why, do see this lot of things, aunt! What in the world is Ella going to do with them?"

"Oh, I know!"

"You know? Then I can guess, and, it is some of your charitable works. You are going to make a juvenile Lady Bountiful of El, eh?"

Ella, who had colored to the roots of her hair at the *exposé* of her very unfashionable Christmas preparations, now took heart, and bestowed a very gentle and salutary little cuff on the saucy head that still wore the purple cap, and then hastened to gather up her various purchases.

"Laugh away," said she, gaily, "and a good many others will laugh, too, over these things. I got them to make people laugh — people that are not in the habit of laughing!"

"Well, well, I see into it," said Will; "and I tell you I think right well of the idea, too. There are worlds of money wasted, at this time of the year, in getting things that nobody wants, and nobody cares for after they are got; and I am glad, for my part, that you are going to get up a variety in this line; in fact, I should like to give you one of these stray leaves to help on," said he, dropping a ten dollar note into her paper. "I like to encourage girls to think of something besides breastpins and sugar candy."

But our story spins on too long. If anybody wants to see the results of Ella's first attempts at *good fairyism,* they can call at the doors of two or three old buildings on Christmas morning, and they shall hear all about it.

Spring Early

Scott Geisel

Christine Everhart just wanted to be left alone. She leaned forward and pedaled harder into the cold Ohio wind. No one asking how she's been, what she's been up to, how she likes being home again. Will she be staying for the holidays? Just ten minutes to herself would do some good. Ten minutes without the questions, without the memories.

The ancient Schwinn three-speed shuddered with her into potholes and over curbs, and the cold bit into Christine's cheeks and settled in her feet and hands. How had she ever done this as a child and thought nothing of it? Had Ohio really always been this cold?

She'd left for college and warmer climates right after high school, took the bus down to Florida with a boy she started dating her senior year in high school. They fell more deeply in love, settled in Jacksonville, and liked it—the warmth, the beach, a city big enough to get lost in. Nothing like here.

Christine loved her family, and so had Mike, and they'd carefully arranged trips for their parents to visit them in Jacksonville. In fifteen years, Christine had only been home twice: once for Mike's funeral, and now because of her grandmother's stroke. Spending Christmas at home was so far proving more challenging than she'd expected.

When Christine rounded the corner from Walnut onto Elm and saw the bright orange cones lining the street in front of the school, she knew she'd made a mistake. Early release. Last day before Christmas break, and they were getting out early, just like when she'd gone to school at Shady Elm Elementary.

A few kids trickled out the doors into the early afternoon sun, and then a flood of color and motion erupted—coats, hats, arms, legs, and book bags fluttering and churning through the school yard toward the crosswalk. Christine dodged another pothole and tried to force the rusted shift level down into first gear. The chain stuttered and popped off the sprocket, and she felt the pedals slip beneath her feet as she skittered to a stop in front of the crosswalk, where the sea of children swallowed her up. This was the opposite of alone.

Christine looked down to examine the damage, and a hand reached through the chatter and giggles to her shoulder. "Do you need some help?" the voice offered. She looked up at Officer McLean. How could he still be on the force? He was old when he'd been manning the school crossing when she was a child.

"No," Christine said, but she waited until the children had crossed and let him walk the bike with her to the curb.

Officer McLean bent to examine the damage. "All rusted up," he said. "I don't know how you were riding this thing."

"Didn't shift," Christine said.

He pulled a Swiss Army knife from his pocket, extracted the screwdriver blade, and wedged the chain loose from the gears on the back tire. "This might get you home," he said. "But I wouldn't go on any cross-country trips."

"I'm headed to Creighton's," she said.

Officer McLean raised an eyebrow. "You don't already have one, you ought to pick up a can of oil while you're there."

⚜ ⚜

Christine thanked him and pushed off down the street. How could she escape her past when it was still alive, all around her, a breathing mass of history?

Creighton's Hardware looked like it always had—small and cramped with narrow aisles, but an amazing array and variety of tools, hardware, and supplies, all arranged so that at least one of each item was visible on a shelf. There were still the pots and pans and kitchen utensils, coffee makers and pressure cookers, and the basement with plumbing supplies, which was ironic because the basement flooded every time there was even a modest rain. And just as Christine had expected, the front window was once again packed full with Christmas decorations, lights, miniature trees, wrapping paper, and gift items. It was ablaze with the holiday.

She took her time picking out one set of white lights and one of blue from the window display, looking through the other items as she did to make mental notes for later. She still hadn't found a gift for her parents. Usually, it was a mail order item—fruit of the month club, something nice for the house, or an item they'd picked out themselves. But with Grandma's stroke and the phone calls and distractions and last-minute travel plans, she hadn't gotten to it yet this year. And with Christmas just a few days away, there wasn't time to have a package sent.

When she turned the corner into the row of electronic supplies, there was something new: John Huston, standing with an elderly woman and explaining how a three-way light bulb worked. He was wearing a red Creighton's apron around his waist and he rung up her order. John smiled when he saw Christine but didn't turn his attention from the woman until she had gone. "Christine," he said, coming from behind the register toward her. "Long time."

His hair was darker than she remembered, and a little thinner at the temples, but he was the same guy she remembered from high school—thin, big ears, and the best smile she'd ever seen. They'd dated before she went with Mike. John had talked about college but dragged his feet. Christine had just wanted to get out, and Mike was ready for that, too. That's the way Christine remembered it.

"Finding everything?" John asked.

"Extension cord," Christine said.

He stepped around her and picked up one from the shelf. "What length?"

"Green," she said. "It has to be green."

He put the cord back and walked down the aisle. "Those are all up front with the Christmas lights."

She followed him, and he reached deep into the display case in the window. "Six feet OK?"

"Fine," she said, and he handed one to her.

"I heard you were in town," he said. "And I'm sorry to hear about your grandma."

Christine flinched. "Jeez, does everyone know everything around here? Everywhere I go, it's like people are expecting me. Everyone knows I'm home. Mom's made the rounds. At the post office, at the bank. I can't buy a banana without someone asking me how I've been or how's Grandma."

John shrugged. "Just like always. So how is she?"

Christine let out a breath. "The same. The stroke hit her right side, and that was her dominant arm, so she's having a hard time adjusting."

John nodded. "She's at home?"

Christine shook her head. "Out of the hospital, but staying with mother and dad. She can't be on her own." It was cozy. She had the basement to herself so Grandma could have her old room upstairs, but it was still less privacy than she was used to.

"I wish her a speedy recovery," John said, then looked thoughtful for a moment. "So no spring earlies this year?"

Christine looked up at him. "Did you say spring early?"

"I did."

"You know they're called springerle, right?" she said, drawing out the *spring* and the *er* and the *lee*.

John laughed. "I've called them that since I was a kid. Your grandmother always sent some cookies to my family, and I always got a few. These past few years she's been sending them to my mother. I still get some. No one else makes spring earlies like your grandmother."

Christine examined the extension cord and lights in her hand. It was true. She still got a box mailed to her every year. They were perfect. A thin crunchy layer on the outside and a soft cakey inside that was so strong with anise the whole house was filled with the scent the day they arrived in the mail.

"Oh, sorry," John said. "Selfish of me. The important thing is your grandma's health."

"No, it's–"

"My apologies," John repeated.

"No–she . . . She had a premonition."

"Oh?"

"Gram made them early. She said she knew something was going to happen, and she baked them in October."

"Right before the stroke?"

Christine nodded. "We have a whole pantry full. They're spilling out everywhere."

"That ought to make her happy."

Christine stood silently. She supposed it did.

"OK, anything else?" John asked.

"Oil," she said. "I need a can of oil."

He started off across the store. "What kind?"

"For my bike chain. It jammed on the way over here."

He picked out a small can and took it to the register. She followed again, and when he'd rung everything up and was putting her things into a bag, he held up the can of oil and asked, "You want me to help you with this? Put some on now?"

She looked at him, puzzled.

"The bike is outside?"

"Why does everyone keep trying to help me? Do I look like I need help?"

John dropped the can into the paper bag and folded the top over. "Sorry," he said, holding up his hands. "That's twice today. I can't afford another one."

"No," Christine said, shaking her head. "It's me. It's just– Look, I'd love some help. It's in the rack out front."

When he got outside and saw the bike, John laughed. "How old is this thing?"

"Old as me," Christine said, already feeling the sting of the cold again on her skin. He wasn't even wearing a coat.

John oiled the chain, the derailleur, the cables, the shifter, and then the chain again, wiping the excess with a rag he'd brought from inside. "It's gonna need brake pads and air in the tires if you want to keep riding it," he said.

Christine pulled her hat down tight, took the can from John, and placed it into the rusted wire basket along with the other items.

"I'll do that," she said, pulling her mittens on. But before she left, she turned again to John. "There's just one thing I don't understand."

"Mm hmm?"

"Why are you working at a hardware store?"

John frowned.

"Why are you still here?" she pressed. "You were so smart. You were going to go away. What happened?"

The frown got deeper. "I'm working here because Mr. Creighton is a family friend. He needs the help. Christmas is actually a very busy time for him, and he's getting older. Plus he needs help organizing for the end-of-the-year inventory count." He stuck his hands in his pockets and turned half away from her, speaking now over his shoulder. "I teach chemistry at Oakdell."

"The comm–"

"Yes, I know. We said we'd never go to a community college. But there's good work to be done here, just the same as anywhere else, you know."

Christine closed her eyes. "No, I—"

But she heard the bell on the door tinkle, and John was already back inside.

❦

The warmth from the kitchen engulfed Christine as she stepped through the kitchen door into her parents' house.

"Did you get the lights?" Mom called from the living room.

"Yes."

"Bring them in here."

Her mother had the couch pulled away from the big window and was hanging ornaments from hooks that were stuck to the glass with little suction cups. With Grandma in the wheelchair, there hadn't been room for a tree this year. Christine recognized many of the items already hanging, but there were several she'd never seen before. There was a bird made out of painted walnut shells and cardboard, a bell made from pipe cleaners, and paper snowflakes that were yellowed and falling apart. There were also some very nice things—little crystal balls, a carved wooden Santa, an angel made of lace.

"Where did these come from?" Christine asked, leaning over the back of the couch. She touched one of the paper snowflakes, and it danced fragilely under her fingertip.

Mom put an arm on her shoulder. "You like them? These were on our tree when I was a kid." She pointed to the walnut bird. "I made that in the second grade." Then she turned the lumpy pipe cleaner bell on its hook. "And your uncle Dave, rest his soul, made this two years later in the same class, in the very same seat where I sat. You grandmother always liked that."

Christine looked at her mother and noticed for the first time since she'd been home these past few days the gray in her hair that she couldn't completely hide anymore, and a thinness in her fingers she didn't remember. Mom didn't look old, but she no longer looked young.

"Why haven't I ever seen them before?" Christine asked.

"They were in your grandma's attic," Mom said. "She asked your dad to bring them down."

Christine must have looked confused, because Mom added, "When you were young, we hung the things you made in school. They're still here." She pointed to the origami bird, the construction paper Santa. The she reached for the lights Christine had brought. "Did you see John at Creighton's?"

"What—you knew?"

"Knew what?"

"That he was working there."

"John's been working there at Christmas for years—since Mr. Creighton fell and broke his ankle hanging the display in the window. He starts as soon as the semester is over." She stretched a string of lights tentatively. "You know he teaches at Oakdell?"

"He told me. Yes."

"It's a good job. They seem to like him there, and his mother told me they're going to–"

"Mom . . ." Christine said, rolling her eyes.

"What?"

She worked at a kink in the line of lights. "Let's just get these up before Grandma wakes up."

They fussed with the lights and the ornaments for a while. Christine's mother was unusually quiet, and that put Christine in a quiet mood, too. When they were both satisfied, Mom went off to the kitchen, and when she refused help getting dinner ready, Christine went to the basement to check in on her work before dinner.

She'd fallen into graphic design in college and built up a steady list of clients after she and Mike both graduated together. At first, it had been practical—he worked a good job with benefits, and she had the flexibility to stay home and grow her business. After the accident, the work became her savior. The insurance money had allowed her to keep the house, but it was the distraction of deadlines and responsibilities that had kept her going. And modern technology had afforded her the solitude she'd grown more and more to need. She logged onto email, found a reply from a client who wanted changes to a design, and worked on them until it was time to eat.

Christine came upstairs to the smell of fresh-baked bread and the sound of Grandma maneuvering herself in the wheelchair with her one good leg. Mom was in the living room adjusting the foot rests on the chair. Christine went in and kissed Grandma on the cheek, then, before she realized what she was doing, did the same for her mother.

"I'll set the table," she offered. As she turned, she noticed the darkness outside and in the room and turned toward the light switch.

"Land sakes," Mom said. "I completely forgot." She turned Grandma to face the window, and Christine flicked the colored lights on. The room came aglow with reflections of twinkling memories.

Grandma squealed, as much as she could with one side of her

face still hampered from the stroke. "Janet," she gurgled, looking at Mom. "You . . . found them."

"They were right where you said." Mom patted Grandma's shoulder. "George brought them down."

And while they admired the window, Christine slipped into the kitchen and began arranging plates and silverware. She didn't like seeing her grandmother struggle. The recovery seemed too slow.

A moment later, Mom pushed Grandma in and nudged her as close to the table as possible, then locked the chair's wheels. "Call your father," she said, and Christine went to the back door and flicked the outside lights, the same signal she'd used since she was a child.

Dad appeared from the garage, and Christine saw the blanket of white beginning to form as he made his way to the house. He stamped his feet on the landing. "Starting to pick up out there," he said. "No sense shoveling until morning." He looked at the front window. "That really looks nice, Ma," he said, and they all sat down to eat.

Meals had been especially difficult for Grandma since the stroke, and tonight was worse than usual. Even with her food cut into small pieces, swallowing was difficult. Dad twice had to get up and gently pound Grandma on the back to clear her throat, and the exertion was clearly tiring for her. Christine watched patiently, wishing there were more she could do.

When the table had been cleared, Christie poured coffee and brought out a tin of springerles from the pantry. Grandma reached out with her good arm and picked one off the top. "Grandma," Christine said, "where did the springerle recipe come from?"

Grandma's eyes lit up. "My great-great-great-great grandma." She drew a breath. "And probably . . . back farther than that." She wiped the corner of her mouth and swallowed hard. "They came over from the old country."

Grandma reached for her coffee—Christine had made her decaf—and Mom helped her take a sip. "We used to . . . you remember my sister Berta, and Ruthie and Mary?"

Christine nodded, and Grandma struggled to clear her throat and get the words out. "Our mothers made them—the old way. They bought bus tickets and we rode to each others' houses. One family . . . would buy the eggs, another one bought . . . the sugar, and another the anise oil and flour." Grandma stopped as they all waited for her to find her place again. "It took two days. The boys beat the eggs. They handed the bowl down . . . from oldest to youngest. When their arms got tired, they'd start again from the top."

Grandma paused, and Christine found herself bending forward, listening. "The men—my father—finished when they got home. Then . . . then we made the molds and let them dry overnight. In the morning—we'd ride the bus again and do the baking. It was—"

Grandma choked, and they all leaned in toward her. "It was glorious!" Grandma stammered. "Glorious."

There was a sparkle in Grandma's eye that Christine hadn't seen for a long time, and she wanted to be that little girl, riding the bus and making the springerles. "I want you to teach me," she said.

Mom looked at her.

"Us," Christine said. "Maybe . . . do you want to—" she started, looking at her mother, but Mom was already shaking her head yes.

Grandma beamed and made a writing motion with her left hand. "Paper," she said. "You'll need a shopping list."

* * *

The snow was shin-deep in the morning, and still falling. Dad grabbed a sweatshirt and work gloves and went out to shovel. Christine put on thermals, jeans, an extra pair of socks, coat and scarf, a hat, and heavy gloves, then followed him. It took about two minutes of shoveling for her to realize she was overdressed.

Dad laughed as she tugged at the scarf and pulled her hat off. "You used to do this without a coat, and your mother would yell at you." Dad pointed to the window. "She's there now."

Christine waved at Mom and lowered the zipper on the front of her coat.

"You'll get me in trouble yet," Dad said, and tossed snow at her.

She laughed and tossed a shovelful back. By the time they'd cleared the driveway, breakfast had turned into brunch, and the snow was still falling, turning everything white again.

As soon as they'd finished eating, Christine put on her coat and hat. Dad looked at her. "Might as well wait a while. It doesn't look like it's going to stop yet."

"No," Christine said. "I'm going to walk to town and get the things for the springerles."

"Why don't you take the car?" Mom offered. "A mile will seem like a long way in the snow."

Christine shook her head. "You know I don't want to drive. Especially in the snow." She'd already emptied her laptop carry case and had it slung over her shoulder.

When she rounded the house, the lights in the front window flashed on. She smiled and plunged into the deep snow at the curb. A few people were just beginning to clear the sidewalks. Walking through the tire tracks carved into the street seemed the best way to travel, and not a single car appeared on the roads until she was almost to the two-lane county road that ran through the center of town.

It was like a party downtown. The Emporium was crowded with people buying coffee, there was an army of kids shoveling the sidewalks in front of the stores, the Boy Scouts were selling wreaths at a table in front of the cinema, and the book mobile was parked at the curb in front of Roger's Market. Nobody seemed to mind the cold or the piles of snow they had to step over and through just to move about.

Christine waded through the market, down the narrow aisles slick with slushy shoeprints, and found everything she'd need for the springerles except one item. She smiled vaguely at the thought of where she'd have to get it, checked out and carefully packed everything into her bag, then treated herself to a cup of coffee before her last stop. While she was at the Emporium, she poured a second cup, then headed across the street to Creighton's.

The library was holding a bake sale in the crowded hardware store, and then Christine remembered. This building had been the site of the town's first library, and every year on the anniversary of its opening, there was a bake sale here and—she turned to look out the window—a book sale in the book mobile. She'd begged Mom to bring her here every Saturday before Christmas.

Christine bought brownies, a couple of cupcakes, and a bag full of cookies and stuffed them all into her bag. She was almost out the door when she remembered what she'd come for, and why she'd been juggling a second cup of coffee.

John was ringing up an order, and she inconspicuously set the coffee and a brownie next to him by the register and kept going. When she came back with a set of metal measuring spoons, the place was temporarily quiet, and he was unwrapping the brownie and looking at her.

"To say I'm sorry," she said. "Yesterday. I didn't mean to . . ."

"I know," John said. "It's just been a while."

"Right. We had some catching up to do."

John leaned onto the counter. "When was the last time you were home?"

Christine saw that he immediately recognized the answer, and wished he hadn't asked. "The funeral," she said, surprised to hear the words come out.

"I didn't mean to . . ." John started.

"Mike's family wanted him buried here."

John held up a hand. "I didn't mean to pry."

Christine was silent for a moment. "I didn't see you there."

John frowned, sighed, set down his brownie and got a serious look on his face. "Look, you know it broke my heart when—"

"When I married Mike, I know."

"What? No, when he died. I know you really loved him. You two loved each other. That's what made it so hard. How could I pay my respects to that? I would have just gotten in the way."

Christine's knees felt soft. "You know I was driving when it happened?"

"I heard that," John said. "And I also heard it was the other driver's fault."

"Everyone kept telling me that," she said. "But it never felt OK."

The door jangled then, and two young boys ran in and excitedly asked John if they could sweep the walk out front, or shovel the curb. He asked if they had their own shovels, and they shook their heads yes and ran back out to work.

He turned back to Christine and picked up the measuring spoons. "You can't tell me your mother doesn't already have a set of these?"

"It's for the anise oil," she said. "It eats through plastic."

He looked quizzical. "But your grandmother already made the spring earlies?"

Christine felt a flush of warmth. "I'm going to learn." She glanced toward the front window display. "And I'm still looking for the perfect gift for Mom and Dad, too. Do you think I might find something here?"

John rang up the sale and tucked the spoons into Christine's bag for her. "They don't need anything else," he said coyly.

❦

Making the springerles took all the rest of that day. Grandma was in the middle of everything, pushing herself around in the wheelchair with her one good leg, sticking her nose into the bowls and checking on everything. Mom and Christine laughed and made a mess, and Dad finished the shoveling once the snow had stopped, then fell asleep in front of the TV.

When it was time to roll the dough, Grandma instructed Mom to get down her rolling pin, and she got very serious. "You know," Grandma said to Christine, "your grandfather carved this rolling pin himself."

Christine looked at the pattern of simple shapes—holly berries, an evergreen, a rudimentary dove. They were indelibly etched in her childhood memories.

"I always stuck . . . some in the back of the freezer for him. For his birthday. He loved–those cookies. And he never could figure out . . . how I had them fresh in the spring."

Christine rolled the pin carefully and watched the shapes emerge in the dough. By the time they'd cut them all apart, laid them out to dry overnight, and eaten dinner and cleaned everything up, Grandma was already long asleep. As Christine was heading down to the basement for the night, she turned to her mother. "Mom, do you know if John Huston ever married?"

Mom kissed Christine on the cheek. "Never," she whispered, and slipped away.

Christine logged onto email to check her work before she turned in, paused, and searched for the Oakdell College chemistry department's web page.

The next morning, they baked. The springerles bloomed perfectly, just like they were supposed to, with the little shapes embossed on the tops. Grandma made sure they were wrapped and sealed tightly. "We didn't have . . . those plastic bags," she said. "If you didn't get a tin of cookies sealed tight, they'd be hard as rocks when you got back to them."

She also made sure that the first batch she'd made stayed separate from this new bunch. "You know," she said, "they're no good for at least three weeks. If you eat them before that . . . the flavor won't . . . go through." She oversaw the whole operation.

Mom told Grandma that she was wearing herself out and should slow down, but Grandma wouldn't have any of that. "This might be my last Christmas," she said. "You'll let an old lady have her due, won't you?"

When the last of the cookies were sealed up, Christine called from the pantry, "There's no room." Springerles were spilling out from the shelves, falling onto Christine as fast as she tried to re-stack them.

"Grandma," she said. "You've got to deliver these. Don't you always give a bunch away?"

Grandma started. "Of course." She lurked forward in her wheelchair. "We've got to get going."

Christine picked up the phone. "Where do we start?"

"The Dickensons," Grandma called. "Seven six seven, five two—"

"Now hold on a minute," Mom said. "Just who's going to be doing the delivering?"

"Both of us," Christine said, looking at Grandma.

"I don't think your grandmother is up to that," Mom said. "And the weather . . ."

"I'm going," Grandma said. "Get my coat."

"I don't think—"

"Let her go, Ma," Dad called from his easy chair in the living room. "Better yet, you all should go. All the women."

Mom didn't look convinced.

"I'll clean the car off and bring it around to the side door," Dad said. "The wheelchair folds up. You can put it in the trunk. Any trouble, you call me from the cell and I'll be there with the truck before you can blink."

Things went abuzz. Mom helped bundle up Grandma, Christine copied a list of names that Grandma recited, and Dad was outside warming up the car. When they had Grandma safely in the front seat, Mom slid into the back and handed Christine the keys. Christine didn't take them.

"It's time you got over this," Mom said. "You won't get over twenty miles an hour."

Christine turned to Dad. "Doesn't get much safer than this," he said, and she took the keys and slid in behind the wheel.

She drove overly cautious, but it came back to her right away. Driving in the snow. Breaking before the turn, keeping the wheels straight, rolling stops when there was no one else coming. Mom handled the phone, calling ahead when they could get an answer, but they made their stops regardless of whether someone was home or not. They went to everyone Grandma could think of— childhood friends who were still alive, or their kids, the senior center, Reverend Martin at the church, Cheryl at the bank. Anyone who had ever shown interest in or eaten Grandma's springerles got some.

The streetlights were coming on as they made their way home, trying to think of anyone they may have missed. As they edged past the cemetery, Christine looked over in the dim light. It was the first time she'd seen this place since they'd had the service for Mike. He hadn't gotten away any more than she had.

And when they pulled into the driveway and she saw the front window all lit up, it came to Christine whom they'd forgotten. She'd have to make one more trip tomorrow.

❦ ⁘ ❦

Grandma was already awake and at the kitchen table in her wheelchair when Christine came up for coffee in the morning. Mom was in the back of the house somewhere, and Dad was nowhere in sight.

Christine filled her mug and sat down next to Grandma. Grandma patted Christine's hand. "Eat some on the thirty-first," she said.

Christine cocked her head.

"March thirty-first. Your grandfather's birthday."

Christine got up and took a bag of springerles from the pantry, wrapped it inside a sandwich bag, and stuck it all the way in the back of the freezer while Grandma watched.

"He always like it when spring came early," Grandma said. "If I'm not here, you remember."

"I will," Christine promised.

Mom came in and they had a light breakfast, then Christine rolled the Schwinn out of the garage and pushed it down the driveway. Smatterings of snow and patches of rough ice glistened on the black pavement. Riding the bike probably wasn't the best idea, but she was going to do it anyway. It would keep her closer to things.

She was dressed in layers now, a windbreaker over her winter coat, scarf loose around her neck. Her old hiking boots dug out from the back of her closet to keep her feet warm. She was learning to adjust. She checked her pockets, looked back once at the house, then slowly pedaled out into the cleanest tracks through the snow in the street.

The gears groaned when she tried to shift, but the chain slipped down into first and she felt a solidness in the pedal. Everything was quiet and bright in the sunlight reflecting off the white snow. The tires squeaked through the frozen ruts, and Christine rode carefully, turning her face from the wind when she could to keep her eyes from watering.

She took her time, and when she reached the school, it was beautifully quiet and pristine. The snow rolled in billowy drifts over the yard. Not a footprint disturbed the scene, and Christine stopped at the curb and looked down along the line of the second-grade wing. Her mother may have forgotten, but Christine had been in Mrs. Kleckner's class too, at the end of her teaching career, and they had also made Christmas ornaments. And then another thought came back to her. That was the classroom where she'd first met John. The past kept threading itself into the future—here, more than anywhere.

She pedaled through the streets past downtown and out toward the cemetery. When she got to the gates, there was a wide open expanse of white in front of her. Another untouched landscape. Though it had been nearly five years since she'd been here and the snow was deep, Christine knew the way. Mike's grave was on the main path, under the wide oak where his family plot lay. She pushed her way there and cleared a spot in front of the headstone.

"For you, Mike," she said, sitting on the granite and pulling out a springerle. She took a bite and savored it as long as she could before it melted away. "You always liked these," she said, scanning the dips and rolls in the snowdrifts. She took another bite and breathed in the scent.

She finished her springerle, then carefully re-sealed the bag and tucked it back into her pocket. "I hope you don't mind," she said. "But there's an old friend I have to go see." She paused, sniffed deeply and drew the cold air down into her lungs, then let it out. "You know him, and you know we dated before you and I got together. That's especially important now. I think you'll understand."

Christine waited quietly, hoping for an answer but knowing it wouldn't come that easily. Then she got up to walk back down to her bike and make her way to the hardware store. Tonight was Christmas Eve, and she had one last batch of springerles to deliver before the spring thaw.

Early Shnoring on Christmas Eve in Akron

Eric Wasserman

My wife Thea and I decided to spend our first Ohio Christmas alone in our first home surrounded by what my mother would call our "early *shnoring*" collection. In Yiddish a *shnorrer* is a beggar who makes pretensions to respectability, a sponger, or a parasite. This is not exactly the most flattering label to bestow upon somebody. But in my family early *shnoring* has mutated into being defined as the accumulation of handed-down items a young married couple such as ourselves receives out of generosity to get their first home started. The early *shnoring* Thea and I have acquired is practical: a dining room table that had been collecting dust in my mother-in-law's rural Indiana shed, end tables and a couch from Thea's stepfather's bachelor days, a hutch from our new neighbors, a coffee table from Thea's father in Boston. The previous owners of our eighty-eight-year-old house even left a beautiful oak church pew in the breakfast nook. "Do you think they're religious?" I had asked Thea when we first saw the home. We are now experienced *shnorrers*. People are always nice when they give us items but the unspoken code of *shnoring* is that they have been wanting an excuse to discard something and we actually need it. So, it's a fair trade.

In addition to *shnoring*, Thea and I are also experts at creating our own rituals. We've always bonded over movies and these rituals often take on a cinematic angle. After we get paid each month we have a dinner and movie date. If we can't afford going out we have a home movie date. Every Passover and Easter season I make her watch Charlton Heston in *The Ten Commandments* and every Fourth of July she insists we bond over Stephen Spielberg's *Jaws*. These rituals are also fair trades.

Blended families can often be complex, but in our case it gets downright convoluted around religious holidays. I'm a recovering Jew, Thea's father is a devout atheist, her mother is a Chinese qigong master, and her stepfather is a Buddhist who still shows tinges of his evangelical upbringing. To one side of our new house lives a pastor and his wife with their four children and to the other is a retired nun. We seem to be covered on all divine fronts. But Thea and I prefer to call the winter holiday season "HanuMas." And as a couple with ambivalent devotion to anything other than each other, we turn to the great American religion of movie watching. Having survived four paycheck-to-paycheck seasonless years in a tiny one-bedroom in Los Angeles before moving to Ohio, what could be more appropriate?

Choosing a movie to watch on Christmas Eve is not a casual process. Our classification of what constitutes a "Christmas movie" is rather vague: the story only has to take place during Christmas. Thea's sensibility usually leans towards *It's a Wonderful Life* while mine is more in line with *Die Hard*. For our first Ohio Christmas I won a children's chocolate Hanukkah *gelt* coin toss and we settled on *Lethal Weapon* (Mel Gibson's anti-Semitism temporarily forgiven in the spirit of the occasion). I let Thea peel away the gold tin and eat the chocolate *gelt* as a consolation prize.

But, before we could indulge in Sergeant Martin Riggs taking on the bad guys in our former Los Angeles haunts, Thea had to spend at least an hour practicing meditation with our two cats. Christmas action movies are, of course, watched best on a peaceful mind. So, as snow lightly dusted our cobblestoned Akron, Ohio neighborhood, I cleaned up all the takeout Chinese boxes we had dug disposable chopsticks into for the past twenty minutes and pocketed the fortune cookie script telling me, "Your dwelling is your solace." My next job was to begin Christmas Eve movie watching preparations. Going for simplicity (or laziness, depending on one's perspective), I decided to postpone arrangements until ten minutes before Thea joined me. I would instead practice my own form of meditation: house work.

When we bought our home, the previous owners were gracious enough to invite us to a neighborhood block party the week before our move-in date and show us all the little quirks of the house. We received a private walk-through, shown everything from how not to snap off the light switches that their children had routinely damaged ("You don't have kids," the husband, Jeff, had said, "they'll break anything") to how to turn on the external gas heater in the finished downstairs TV room. When we came into the basement corner we saw the remains of an old roll top writer's desk—the same kind I had watched my father pay bills from as a child back in Oregon. It was mostly intact but with several pieces scattered atop or resting on the concrete floor. When I said that I was a writer and the desk looked like my father's, Jeff turned to me and asked, "Would you like to keep it?" Several thoughts immediately surfaced. Yes, of course I really wanted it. No, I would not look forward to salvaging it. And the city boy in me wondered if we would need to get our real estate agents involved to protect either of us from lawyering up over it in the future even though Jeff was an attorney. Then again, it was obvious he hadn't done anything with the desk and maybe he was looking for an excuse to get it off his hands. Which is, of course, the catch of the early *shnoring* relationship. "It belonged to my grandfather, Benjamin Floyd James," he said.

This ignited the emergence of all of Thea's Midwestern-bred manners. She said, "Oh, we couldn't take it then," knowing full well I wanted it. I had observed this ritual many times but had yet to master it (still haven't). As Thea has explained to me, Midwestern protocol requires that when such an offer is made a polite consideration for the owner's feelings is given without necessarily declining the gift. Then, the owner is to reaffirm his generosity and the item can be accepted (an Akron native recently told me that this ritual is intensified if one is Catholic). My fear here was that Thea had activated stage two of this Midwestern protocol and Jeff might not instigate stage three.

"Jeff," his wife, Judy, asked, "are you sure you want to give that away?" My hopes had been crushed.

Jeff looked at me and smiled. He could tell I wanted it. "It's time, Judy." I'd eventually be given an early *shnoring* computer desk from Judy as well for my upstairs office. Then he said to me, "Consider it a welcome-in gift to our home." He patted me on the shoulder and proceeded to instruct me how to evacuate water from annual basement flooding, making me want to race back to our apartment on Casterton to double-check the insurance coverage I had just secured. "Don't worry," Jeff said, "I'm going to leave you my e-mail and phone number in case you have any questions about our house. Or if you need a lawyer," he joked.

That first Christmas Eve in our new home, as my wife meditated surrounded by our cats in our attic bedroom, I passed through the living room cluttered with menorahs and dreidels on the mantel sent by my mother and stockings hanging over the fireplace as I drank black coffee from a mug with the words "Fine . . . I evolved, you didn't" across the ceramic that my atheist father-in-law had given us. I walked by the Chinese protection amulet Thea's mother had sent from one of her qigong retreats in China and made my way downstairs, thinking of my parents back in Oregon eating takeout Chinese with all their Jewish friends.

The finished downstairs room Jeff built himself was chilly. I knew Thea would want the external gas heater turned on, but I'm cheaper than ice water and left it off. I was wearing a sweater. Good enough. I had planned on doing laundry but I stopped. There against the wall was Jeff's grandfather's desk, completely restored. I stood for a moment and stared at it—proud.

Two weeks earlier I had opened the door to the basement, flicked on the light and there in the corner was the dilapidated roll top writing desk covered by dust. I had taken all of the random pieces not attached and placed them in the TV room, then went to move the desk base itself. It not only weighed too much to lift, it was too wide to push through the door Jeff had constructed between the basement and the room he finished. After a quick assessment I saw that I could likely take the desk base apart with a screwdriver, move all the parts into the TV room, and then reconstruct it.

The roll top and top-drawer sections had come off the easiest. But the base and main drawer sections seemed to be interconnected and secured to three or four other pieces. It was sturdy alright. We wanted to buy an older house because we felt the cliché was true that "they don't make them like they used to." The desk proved to be the same. As my thumb and forefinger gradually numbed from twisting the screwdriver counterclockwise, I realized none of the sections were coming apart as the pile of rusty screws on the basement concrete multiplied. I then got on my back and scooted under to take a look at the backboard. It seemed all the base pieces reverted to it, but there was only one large backboard screw. Counterclockwise screwdriver turn, rust flaking off as it slowly emerged, sticking to my wedding band. One more turn, just one more.

The sound I heard before the entire desk fell apart and the base pieces came crashing down on me had been like the ping of a thin metal rod lightly tapping a triangle when I was in the percussion section of junior high school orchestra. What followed was more like the sound of firewood logs tumbling from a poorly arranged stack in the backyard. When I opened my eyes, already convinced my face was now so disfigured nobody would recognize me from my wedding pictures, I found the desktop resting on my chest with the backboard behind my head and all the other base components and rusty screws littered to my sides. Not a scratch, only my chest feeling like one of my brothers had sucker-punched me when we were kids.

"What the hell are you doing down there?" Thea shouted from upstairs. Then I heard her socked feet on the floors above followed by the sound of paws. The desktop had not been terribly difficult to move off my chest. I picked myself up as I heard Thea enter the kitchen saying, "I'll start the popcorn." We, of course, had a home movie date that night.

I decided it was fruitless to attempt cleaning up before she got downstairs, but one of the base drawer sections had lodged between the basement and the TV room. I would take just that one piece into the finished room and call it a night. I bent down and took it in my arms, and was halfway into the finished room when the bottom completely fell out. A smaller tumbling wood stack sound. This time on my Nikes.

"What on earth are you doing?" Thea called again.

I looked down and could see that this section was not solid. It had two smaller compartments. I went to take each piece when I noticed something sticking out of one of the small inner slots. I bent down and tweezed tan paper between my thumb and forefinger. It was a dusty booklet the size and thickness of a poker playing card stack. I could only hope for priceless baseball cards. When I opened it I found a collection of sepia-toned photographs glued together at the booklet's spine. There were women in dresses and men in military uniforms from long before I was born. I figured they had to have been taken in the forties or fifties.

I heard Thea coming down the stairs from the kitchen, turned and saw her stop. She was holding the popcorn bowl, staring back and forth between the pile of desk parts in the TV room and the now fractured base beyond the basement door. She looked at me and grinned. "Was this really necessary, tonight?" I decided not to mention my near death experience and didn't answer. "Hey, what's that you're holding?" She descended the rest of the stairs, saying, "God it's freezing down here. Turn on the gas heater." We had yet to use it. I held out the little photo booklet and fanned out the pictures. "Where did you get those?"

"They fell out of a trap compartment in the desk, just like a *Hitchcock* film."

Thea cocked her head and made her neck-length brown hair flop to the side in the way I've always found adorable. I love to make movie references. Sometimes they just materialize naturally.

Other times I do it intentionally so I can see Thea's cute reactions. "Who are they of?"

"I don't know, I assume Jeff's family since it was his grandfather's desk."

"What are you going to do with them?" I shrugged. "You should tell them you found them." It seemed obvious, but she was right. "And turn on that gas heater." Thea bundled herself in a blanket with the cats underneath on one of the early *shnoring* green corduroy La-Z-Boys her stepfather had relinquished to us. I went to the small external heater and, just as I remembered Jeff had shown me, opened the gas line and turned the pressure knob clockwise.

Twenty minutes later I was still attempting to turn it on. Just as I was about to kick the heater Thea said, "I smell gas, do you?"

I did.

The image of the house we just bought exploding along with the two of us and the cats after taking out a hefty mortgage instantly materialized. I was convinced I would never be able to pay off the place, but its utter annihilation—home owner's insurance be damned—was unacceptable. "Do you think we should call the gas company?" I asked.

A fifteen-minute debate ensued while the odor increased to the point where we thought we should open windows. Thea finally suggested, "Why not call Jeff; he said we could if we had trouble with anything."

"He was just being nice," I said. "He didn't really mean it."

"It's Ohio, get used to it, city boy." Thea always calls me "city boy" when she wants me to do something, knowing it will compel me to do it.

Just as I was ascending the stairs to find Jeff's phone number, we heard a knock on the front door. Thea and I stared at each other.

"Maybe it's another one of the neighbors with some sort of welcome-to-the-neighborhood basket," she said. We had already collected enough fruit and nuts and cookies to compete with our early *shnoring* enterprise. I went to the front door. Jeff was standing there, as if he had magically appeared in response to our panicking.

"Hey, guy!" he said and put out his hand. "I just stopped by to see if any mail has come for us."

I had the feeling he really wanted to see how his house looked now that we were living in it. And I had indeed been collecting a healthy pile of his mail. But I literally grabbed him two-handed by his extended arm and dragged him inside, his eyes popping with bewilderment. "We need you right now!" I said. Thea emerged from the downstairs, still wrapped in a blanket minus the cats. She looked at Jeff with relief and told him everything.

"You don't need to call the gas company," he said in that pleasant Ohioan manner that lets one save face when essentially being told you've been foolish. It's one of the little pleasantries I truly enjoy about living here. Jeff immediately showed me that I had to also push the pressure knob down while turning clockwise to ignite the pilot of the heater, a minor detail I had forgotten. When I asked about the smell of gas he simply said the line was open for a while without the pilot lit. Thea stared at me and we both felt stupid, but Jeff hadn't made us feel so. And he had made no mention of his grandfather's desk scattered about the TV room in pieces.

"Love the lamp," he said as we emerged from the downstairs and walked into the living room near the fireplace, the spot where Judy had told us their son Cary had taken his first steps. The lamp was actually one of the few items we hadn't *shnored*. "Great, you have your stuff in here and are making it your own. You two remind me so much of Judy and me when we bought the place. How long have you been married?" After a quick rundown of how Thea had turned me down three times for a date before going out with me, we told him, then added that we had had a very quiet wedding with our parents when we finally moved to Akron, followed by dinner at Lanning's Restaurant on Cleveland Massillon Road. "I took Judy there for prom!" he said, excited. It was the beginning of what I have now come to know as the Akron, Ohio one degree of separation.

"Oh, your mail," I said. "It's upstairs."

"Great, let's see what you've done with the place."

I retrieved the mail in my study from Judy's old computer desk, but Thea was already showing Jeff our library room. "This used to be the nursery for each of our kids," Jeff said, perusing the bookshelves now lining the baby blue walls. Then he entered Thea's office and stopped cold. "Oh my God, we forgot to take my daughter Anna's desk with us." The piece of furniture in question was in the corner, a beautiful oak antique children's foldout desk (another early *shnoring* acquisition).

"Oh, it was my mother's," Thea said.

Jeff smiled. "It's practically the same desk and you put it in the identical place we had Anna's. You see, it was meant to be that you would live in our house."

When Jeff left I told Thea, "That was odd, him just showing up like that, even though it was perfect timing."

She shrugged. "It's Ohio." Now, can we have our movie date?"

"I'll make more popcorn." Thea smiled, then paused. "What?" I asked.

"You forgot to tell Jeff about the pictures."

❧ ∴ ❧

That first Christmas Eve in Ohio I stood looking at the roll top desk. The day after Jeff had left two weeks before I had sent him an e-mail: "Hey, I found some old pictures in your grandfather's desk when I was putting it back together. They look at least 50+ years old. I'll keep them safe."

With Thea meditating, I abandoned the idea of doing laundry and went back upstairs and sat at the dining room table her mother gave us. Sipping my coffee, I thought about how far away from the west coast I was (oceans are not that convenient in Ohio). I reached out and took the booklet of pictures I had found in Jeff's grandfather's desk. There's something about old photographs I've always loved. Not just ones of my own family, but aged pictures in general. When looking at them I see the faces and the fashion and the settings and no matter where or when they were taken they always seem to transform into my family. Old photographs have always produced a sense of wonder in me. For some, they are reminders of what to forget. For me, they instill a curiosity for what I never knew.

As I looked at the photo booklet I realized that the people in the pictures did not look too different from my own family. A young man in a uniform with his arm around a pretty girl in a dress could have easily been my grandparents just after WWII broke out. A man in a tweed hat with a feather in the brim might have been the great uncle I was named after. I wondered if the pictures had been taken in Ohio, assumed so.

And then there was the feel of the booklet. I wondered just how old it was, if there were once thirty-three-year-old hands like my own upon them, whose fingertips had held delicately to the edges as to not smudge the images. I wondered what it was like when the film was dropped off at the developer, the anticipation of the photographer seeing the prints. I wondered what the person who picked up the pictures felt seeing them for the first time, what it was like sharing them with those who had shared the original experience.

Of all the places I have lived in my life, Ohio seems to be the only one that really reminded me of home in Oregon (people holding doors for you when you approach a building is more appealing than one might consider). But right then, on Christmas Eve, although it was not my own holiday, it was a time to be with family and mine were over half a continent away. Yet those pictures somehow became my absent family for a moment. My family was instantly with me in Akron, Ohio. I saw my brothers and their wives and children. I saw my aunts and uncles and cousins and grandparents. And I saw my parents. I stared long at one of the pictures—a man in a checkered shirt and suspenders who looked no older than me who was probably in his eighties by now or no longer in the world. I stared at him and could hear my own father shouting from the front door of my childhood house that he was home, that it was Christmas Eve and he had takeout Chinese for everyone and we were going to set up the eight millimeter film projector and watch home movies as a family, that he had had a few three-minute reels developed just for the night. I could see myself in one of those reels, playing with *Star Wars* action figures on shag-green carpet. But it was no longer Oregon; it was now Ohio, where I was planting permanent roots.

I took a sip of coffee as I heard Thea coming down the stairs. I looked over my shoulder as she turned from the living room holding our oldest black Bombay cat in her arms.

"Happy HanuMas." She kissed my cheek. "Ready to watch the anti-Semite kick some Christmas butt?"

Thea fed the cats as popcorn popped in the microwave and I worked the cork out of a bottle of Duck Pond Cellars merlot (a little taste of Oregon for the evening) I had bought at West Point Market on West Market Street. As she entered the kitchen from the breakfast nook to toss the empty Friskies can into the sink, the phone rang.

"It's probably my mother," Thea said. "I should have called her earlier."

On the third ring I answered.

It was Jeff.

"Hey, guy, I got your e-mail," he said. "Am I catching you at a bad time?" It was Christmas Eve, but it wasn't a bad time. I told him that we were spending it alone in the house and were going to watch a movie. "That's great. I remember our first Christmas in the house. Funny story, I'll have to tell it to you sometime. Hey, if it's not too inconvenient, do you mind if I stop by now to get those pictures you found? I'd love to show them to everyone at dinner tonight." I looked over to our *shnored* dining room table and saw the little booklet resting on top of one of Thea's gluten-free cookbooks. I told him it was no problem. "Great, I'll be right over." I asked him if he needed directions. He laughed and said he would see us soon.

I joined Thea in the kitchen where she was scooping Häagen-Dazs chocolate into a bowl. I told her I didn't mind Jeff coming over, I liked him a lot, but it was a bit odd since it was Christmas Eve. Thea just shrugged and said, "It's the Midwest."

When the knock on the door came—this one expected—I was excited. Maybe it was the idea of being able to give Jeff the Christmas gift of those pictures. Maybe it was just inviting somebody into my new home on Christmas Eve even for just a few minutes—even if the house was more familiar to him than it was to us.

When I opened the door, Jeff was standing with a young girl.

"Eric, this is my daughter, Anna." We said hello and I invited them in. Thea offered coffee to Jeff. He declined. "The place is looking good," Jeff said, gazing about the front room. I had finally hung things on the walls since his heater and mail visit, mostly inherited artwork my grandmother had painted (not exactly *shnored*). Anna was already through the living room, snow melting on the shoulders of her winter coat. She walked slowly toward the back entrance to the breakfast nook. I noticed how she held her hands together in front of her coat buttons as she slowly turned her head here and there, seeing our things on the walls of her childhood home. Some of the furniture was in the same places. Our *shnored* couch was in front of the fireplace, but it wasn't her couch. We had a similar antique clock that was my grandmother's, but it was a bit different from the one her parents had displayed. When she finally unclasped her hands I saw her put one palm on the corner of the church pew left for us (not *shnored*, part of the sale).

Thea went to her. "Is it odd seeing the house this way?"

"Yeah, it's strange" Anna said, not to Thea, more to the staircase leading to the upstairs where her bedroom had been transformed into our library that was filled with shelves we actually bought on sale at the Target on West Market Street.

"Wanna see your grandfather's desk?" I asked Jeff.

We left Anna and Thea and I led him down the stairs he had built himself from the kitchen to the TV room. As we descended the stairs he told me how his now college-age son Cary watched him construct them from the top of the kitchen as an infant.

"Fantastic!" he said, seeing the desk restored. I instantly feared that he would now want it back. But he simply pulled out all the little drawers slowly, one by one, and lifted the roll top, smiling. He then looked to the floor beside it. "Hey, you took that from the basement." He was referring to a long shelf I was convinced had been part of the kitchen before it was remodeled that I had pulled from near the washing machine to store my vinyl records. But he was really staring at Hello People's *The Handsome Devils* record he had left. He said casually, "If you ever transfer that album to CD I want a copy; they were the opening act when my brother took me to see Janis Joplin." I decided not to ask what year that was, but it was cool to know that I had moved to a place where Janice Joplin had once performed. "The desk looks great. Now, let me see those pictures."

As we ascended the stairs Jeff told me, "I wasn't all that concerned about retrieving the photos, but Judy insisted. She's the archivist/librarian/family historian and plans to take them to work and re-humidify and flatten them." When we came into the dining room we found Thea and Anna talking.

I went to our *shnored* table and handed over the tiny booklet. Jeff opened it, began to grin and took a seat at the table. "Anna, come take a look," he said. She stood behind his shoulder. "I've never seen any of these." He began to point. "Those are my aunts and uncles in Mississippi. And those are my grandparents. Hey, that's a great one of my grandfather." He looked up at me, winked and returned to the pictures.

"Dad," Anna said, "I'm sure they want to have their first Christmas in the house alone." I couldn't help notice that the pattern of her speech was very much like her mother's when Judy had asked Jeff if he really wanted to give me the desk.

Jeff turned to me. "Oh, our first Christmas in this house was really funny." Anna had that look all children have when their parents are about to tell a story they've heard too many times to count. "It was 1983, before I was a lawyer. I was working at O'Neil's Department Store as an associate credit manager, so I had to stay until six-thirty at night or so—yeah, on Christmas Eve.

My whole family went to a Chinese restaurant. It's our own sort of ritual." Anna then gave her father a look as if to say, Yeah Dad, that's where we're supposed to be now. But I was thinking of my parents and fingered that fortune cookie script in my pocket. "I met everyone at the restaurant instead of going home first," Jeff continued. "My brother and his family had arrived here from Dallas that day, so after dinner we took them to see the new house. Judy must have left the house without making sure the front door was latched. We didn't have a storm door then. There was a terrible blizzard and the front door had blown open. We had a dog and two cats then." Thea and I also had two cats and my want for a dog was already an ongoing discussion. "We found all the pets huddled together upstairs trying to stay warm. The house was like an igloo; in fact, the water in the pets' bowls was frozen. It took over twenty-four hours and cost us about a hundred bucks in gas to heat it back up. When I came downstairs on Christmas morning it was still chilly. Funny, huh? Not then, though." Jeff looked back at the pictures. "God, these are great."

"Dad," Anna said softly.

Jeff looked up adoringly at his daughter, then back to us. He stood. "Well, it'll be great showing these to everyone at dinner."

"Don't send any blizzards to our door while you're eating Chinese," I said and smiled.

Jeff smiled back.

As I came into the TV room after walking Jeff and Anna out I could already hear Thea singing along to Bobby Helms' rendition of "Jingle Bell Rock" as the opening credits of *Lethal Weapon* came over images of the downtown Los Angeles skyline we had left behind after I was offered my position at The University of Akron. She handed me my wine and held out the popcorn bowl. I took a handful, noticing that our large black Bombay cat was sleeping next to Thea's grandfather's miniature Monon Hoosier Line train set left to us when her grandmother died, our calico on her lap. I decided to take a seat on the floor next to Jeff's grandfather's desk—his *shnoring* gift to us. The warmth from the external gas heater felt nice. I glanced at the desk that looked like the one my father used to pay bills from when I was a child. Then I thought of how Dad was the one who took me to all of the *Lethal Weapon* movies growing up and imagined him at a Chinese restaurant in Portland with my mother and their friends, just like Jeff and Anna were heading to. But I was in Ohio, and it felt wholly right for the first time since coming here.

I finally looked at Thea and said, "Happy HanuMas."

We tapped wine glasses.

She smiled, leaned over, and kissed my cheek. "You, too."

An Old-Time Christmas

Paul Laurence Dunbar

When the holidays came round the thoughts of 'Liza Ann Lewis always turned to the good times that she used to have at home when, following the precedent of anti-bellum days, Christmas lasted all the week and good cheer held sway. She remembered with regret the gifts that were given, the songs that were sung to the tinkling of the banjo and the dances with which they beguiled the night hours. And the eating! Could she forget it? The great turkey, with the fat literally bursting from him; the yellow yam melting into deliciousness in the mouth; or in some more fortunate season, even the juicy 'possum grinning in brown and greasy death from the great platter.

In the ten years she had lived in New York, she had known no such feast-day. Food was strangely dear in the Metropolis, and then there was always the weekly rental of the poor room to be paid. But she had kept the memory of the old times green in her heart, and ever turned to it with the fondness of one for something irretrievably lost.

That is how Jimmy came to know about it. Jimmy was thirteen and small for his age, and he could not remember any such times as his mother told him about. Although he said with great pride to his partner and rival, Blinky Scott, "Chee, Blink, you ought to hear my ol' lady talk about de times dey have down w'ere we come from at Christmas; N'Yoick ain't in it wid dem, you kin jist bet." And Blinky, who was a New Yorker clear through with a New Yorker's contempt for anything outside of the city, had promptly replied with a downward spreading of his right hand, "Aw fu'git it!"

Jimmy felt a little crest-fallen for a minute, but he lifted himself in his own estimation by threatening to "do" Blinky and the cloud rolled by.

'Liza Ann knew that Jimmy couldn't ever understand what she meant by an old-time Christmas unless she could show him by some faint approach to its merrymaking, and it had been the dream of her life to do this. But every year she had failed, until now she was a little ahead.

Her plan was too good to keep, and when Jimmy went out that Christmas eve morning to sell his papers, she had disclosed it to him and bade him hurry home as soon as he was done, for they were to have a real old-time Christmas.

Jimmy exhibited as much pleasure as he deemed consistent with his dignity and promised to be back early to add his earnings to the fund for celebration.

When he was gone, 'Liza Ann counted over her savings lovingly and dreamed of what she would buy her boy, and what she would have for dinner on the next day. Then a voice, a colored man's voice, she knew, floated up to her. Some one in the alley below her window was singing "The Old Folks at Home."

"All up an' down the whole creation, Sadly I roam, Still longing for the old plantation, An' for the old folks at home."

She leaned out of the window and listened and when the song had ceased and she drew her head in again, there were tears in her eyes—the tears of memory and longing. But she crushed them away, and laughed tremulously to herself as she said, "What a reg'lar ol' fool I'm a-gittin' to be." Then she went out into the cold, snow-covered streets, for she had work to do that day that would add a mite to her little Christmas store.

Down in the street, Jimmy was calling out the morning papers and racing with Blinky Scott for prospective customers; these were only transients, of course, for each had his regular buyers whose preferences were scrupulously respected by both in agreement with a strange silent compact.

The electric cars went clanging to and fro, the streets were full of shoppers with bundles and bunches of holly, and all the sights and sounds were pregnant with the message of the joyous time. People were full of the holiday spirit. The papers were going fast, and the little colored boy's pockets were filling with the desired coins. It would have been all right with Jimmy if the policeman hadn't come up on him just as he was about to toss the "bones," and when Blinky Scott had him "faded" to the amount of five hard-earned pennies.

Well, they were trying to suppress youthful gambling in New York, and the officer had to do his duty. The others scuttled away, but Jimmy was so absorbed in the game that he didn't see the "cop" until he was right on him, so he was "pinched." He blubbered a little and wiped his grimy face with his grimier sleeve until it was one long, brown smear. You know this was Jimmy's first time.

The big blue-coat looked a little bit ashamed as he marched him down the street, followed at a distance by a few hooting boys. Some of the holiday shoppers turned to look at them as they passed and murmured, "Poor little chap; I wonder what he's been up to now." Others said sarcastically, "It seems strange that 'copper' didn't call for help." A few of his brother officers grinned at him as he passed, and he blushed, but the dignity of the law must be upheld and the crime of gambling among the newsboys was a growing evil.

Yes, the dignity of the law must be upheld, and though Jimmy was only a small boy, it would be well to make an example of him. So his name and age were put down on the blotter, and over against them the offence with which he was charged. Then he was locked up to await trial the next morning.

"It's shameful," the bearded sergeant said, "how the kids are carryin' on these days. People are feelin' pretty generous, an' they'll toss 'em a nickel er a dime fur their paper an' tell 'em to keep the change fur Christmas, an' foist thing you know the little beggars are shootin' craps er pitchin' pennies. We've got to make an example of some of 'em."

'Liza Ann Lewis was tearing through her work that day to get home and do her Christmas shopping, and she was singing as she worked some such old song as she used to sing in the good old days back home. She reached her room late and tired, but happy. Visions of a "wakening up" time for her and Jimmy were in her mind. But Jimmy wasn't there.

"I wunner whah that little scamp is," she said, smiling; "I tol' him to hu'y home, but I reckon he's stayin' out latah wid de evenin' papahs so's to bring home mo' money."

Hour after hour passed and he did not come; then she grew alarmed. At two o'clock in the morning she could stand it no longer and she went over and awakened Blinky Scott, much to that young gentleman's disgust, who couldn't see why any woman need make such a fuss about a kid. He told her laconically that "Chimmie was pinched fur t'rowin' de bones."

She heard with a sinking heart and went home to her own room to walk the floor all night and sob.

In the morning, with all her Christmas savings tied up in a handkerchief, she hurried down to Jefferson Market court room. There was a full blotter that morning, and the Judge was rushing through with it. He wanted to get home to his Christmas dinner. But he paused long enough when he got to Jimmy's case to deliver a brief but stern lecture upon the evil of child-gambling in New York. He said that as it was Christmas Day he would like to release the prisoner with a reprimand, but he thought that this had been done too often and that it was high time to make an example of one of the offenders.

Well, it was fine or imprisonment. 'Liza Ann struggled up through the crowd of spectators and her Christmas treasure added to what Jimmy had, paid his fine and they went out of the court room together.

When they were in their room again she put the boy to bed, for there was no fire and no coal to make one. Then she wrapped herself in a shabby shawl and sat huddled up over the empty stove.

Down in the alley she heard the voice of the day before singing:

"Oh, darkies, how my heart grows weary, Far from the old folks at home."

And she burst into tears.

Old Treasures

Jane Ann Turzillo and Mary Turzillo

Deputy Sgt. Thomas Winfield took one last look at his spit-shine shoes, boosted his gun belt and climbed behind the wheel of his cruiser. He slammed the door, looked over at the empty passenger seat and drummed his fingers on the steering wheel.

It was Christmas Eve and he supposed his partner, Ray, had wheedled off early just like he did Thanksgiving to go home, be with his family. Well, that was fine as far as Winfield was concerned. He'd rather patrol alone. He didn't want to hear about the Play Station 3 games Ray bought his kids or the useless, sentimental locket he bought his wife. Best of all, Winfield could leave the FM radio off so he didn't have to listen to carols.

No, Ray didn't have to worry about approaching him for the night off, Winfield thought. He and Ray had been partners for twelve years and there were no secrets or minced words between the two. Winfield would be happy alone in the cruiser with nothing but the police radio and the quiet snowfall. In fact, he had volunteered to work a double shift.

He watched in his side mirror as Ray came out of the station, Kel-lite in hand and a grin on his face. As Ray got into the cruiser, Winfield tested the red and blue overheads and siren. He took out his tuning forks and began to calibrate the radar.

"I see you've got the old Christmas spirit. Going to run radar on Christmas Eve," said Ray.

"Lot of people drink on Christmas Eve. Law operates tonight same as any other night. Makes no difference to me."

"As many years as I've known you, I will never understand why you hate Christmas so much."

"Did you ever try to get anything done this time of year? For the entire month before Christmas and until after New Year's people are obsessed. The stores become jungles. It's like a month of full moons. Brings out the shoplifters, muggers, con artists . . . More people 'off' themselves during the holidays than any other time of year."

"Been up to see your grandfather yet?"

The question gave Winfield pause, made his blood boil. "Haven't seen him in two months and don't plan on seeing him for another two months." Winfield controlled his anger as he steered the cruiser toward the main streets of the town.

"He's alone. He's old. And it's Christmas."

"That's right. He's old. And he gets on my nerves. We've been through this before."

"Don't you think you owe it to the old man?"

"Owe him?" Winfield looked at his partner incredulously. "You know, you've gone soft, a real bleeding heart. Worries me."

"He raised you after your mother died, didn't he? I think that counts for something."

"I think I'd almost rather hear you sing Christmas carols. Or no! Better yet, tell me all about how Santa's coming to your house tonight." Winfield forced a laugh, but his temper was getting away from him.

"Did you even bother to send him a present?"

That did it! "For crying out loud. You're fine the rest of the year, but in December you become a combination of the ghost of Christmas past and one of Santa's elves. I'm surprised you don't ask me what I got my ex-wife and kid for Christmas."

"That's it, isn't it? You can't face your grandfather. Ever since Diane walked out ten years ago and took Tommy. You lost track of them, and you take it out on everybody and everything. I never knew anybody so filled with bitterness, so cynical. You know what? I think it affects your job."

Winfield ground his teeth. "My job is just fine. It's the rest of these morons we're dealing with on the streets. And why do you bring up my ex-wife? Women. Humph! All the same."

"The ones you're attracted to are."

Winfield turned down the heater. He ran his finger around the inside of his collar. "We're out here to fight crime and suppress evil, not to discuss my morals. Now, do you want the rest of the night off, so you can put on your funny red suit and go slide down the chimney, or don't you?"

"May as well drop me at the station. If I have to ride with you much longer, I might lose my Christmas spirit."

Winfield finished the three p.m. to eleven p.m. shift and patrolled on into the night. The roads got slick from the steady snowfall, but few cars ventured out. Everything was closed except the Convenient Mart, dubbed the "Stop 'n Rob" by the police. Much to Winfield's chagrin even the donut shop was dark. The dispatcher gave him two calls. One was an abandoned auto, the other an injured animal that was gone on his arrival. He made his rounds checking businesses for open doors and flashing his spotlight on darkened homes.

The conversation between he and his partner, Ray, gnawed at him. He thought about Christmas, his grandfather, Diane and his son, Tommy. Ray called him cynical, said his outlook affected his job. Winfield pushed them all from his mind and congratulated himself for being negative. Expect nothing good, then the bad is easier to take," he said aloud.

Things were too quiet. He was getting bored. Something had to happen, or he was going to fall asleep.

About two a.m. he got his wish, a call from the dispatcher to check for a juvenile at the Convenient Mart. Delighted with the prospect of some action—a confrontation with a kid—he felt his adrenalin pump. This could even be a robbery, in which case he would need back up.

The juvenile turned out to be a boy about twelve, downing a bottle of pop while the clerk kept an eye on him.

"Isn't it a little late for you to be out?" Winfield asked.

The youth turned his smooth face up to Winfield. As he did, his mass of shaggy dark hair fell away from his forehead and revealed mischievous dark eyes. "Guess I'll be going home soon."

"Yes. Because I'm going to take you home."

"I knew you would."

Winfield turned to the clerk. "How long has he been here?"

"Came in just a while ago."

Winfield scrutinized the kid. He looked young, but there was something very old about him. "What's your name?"

"Luke."

"What are you doing out so late on Christmas Eve, Luke?"

"Got business, cop." It was the boy's turn to size up Winfield.

"I just bet you do. Where are your parents?"

"Gone. On a trip."

"Who are you staying with?"

"Staying at my mother and step-father's house with my real father."

"You still haven't told me what you're doing out at this hour on Christmas Eve."

"Maybe I'm here to teach you a lesson, cop."

"Talk like that'll get you a trip back to the station instead of to your dad's house."

"OK. If you don't like that explanation, how about—I'm out trying to sneak up on Santa Claus. Like that better?"

Winfield didn't dare smile. The kid had quite a mouth on him, but the cynical cop liked him for some reason. Too lazy to fill out reams of paperwork, Winfield decided to make out an F.I. card on him, load him in the cruiser, and take him home.

"I don't want to go home."

Winfield's eyebrows shot up. "Oh? Why?"

"My old man's a bore."

"Don't you want to get your gifts in the morning?"

"I don't get gifts. I am a gift."

"All right, kid, let's go." Winfield shook his head all the way out to the cruiser, wondering whether kids developed disrespect or inherited it. He was amused by the boy, but uncomfortable about him.

Inside the cruiser Winfield looked at Luke. "Did you run away because your folks are gone?"

"See, I like to go out late at night. I don't like going out during the day and dealing with all these messed up people. And the closer it gets to Christmas, the more messed up they get. Know what I mean?"

Winfield ran his finger around inside his collar. "Yeah, I know what you mean. Tell me where you live."

"Farm down off Temple Road. Hey, do I get the lights and sirens?"

"No. I'm sure your dad's worried about you."

"So what?"

"What a time to run away." Winfield's Adam's apple bulged when he swallowed. "It's Christmas."

Luke's mature eyes were shining. "Why not?"

"Well," Winfield stalled, "I sure wouldn't want my kid to run off on Christmas."

"Maybe you're nice to your kid."

Winfield flushed with anger and long buried pain. "I haven't seen my kid in ten years!"

The boy turned a suddenly amazed face toward him. "Ten years! Hey, did he run away, too?"

"None of your business." Winfield was disgusted with himself for letting the boy goad him.

"Hey, cop, tell me you didn't pull any of this stuff when you were a kid. Didn't you cut out sometimes?"

"My gramps would have killed me," Winfield remarked tersely.

"Your gramps? Your gramps raised you? I don't have a gramps."

"You don't know what you're missing," Winfield remarked sourly, mostly to himself.

"What's he like?"

"Old."

"He still give you presents?"

"Nah."

"Think he might like another kid around. Maybe he'd give me presents."

Winfield tried to control his hostility. "Nah. He got fed up with family stuff and the one grandson he had."

"How come you don't like him?"

"None of your business!" Winfield was almost tempted to try to explain, though he couldn't think for the life of him why. Explain how the old fool always took Diane's side, even when she threatened to leave, even when she took Tommy, the only great-grandson he'd ever have, and left for New Mexico? Texas? Who knew? Worse was the moralizing. Gramps nagged about the steady stream of "cheap" women and the rotten treatment Winfield gave the only sincere woman to ever enter his life. Stupid, old moralizing fool. Winfield didn't want to admit to himself even if the old fool was right. Even if, as Gramps said, the lectures were really for the younger man's own good.

Roughly, Winfield changed the subject. "You don't even have a hat."

"Forgot it, I guess. So, tell me just what you think is so great about Christmas."

Winfield suddenly felt his nightstick jabbing him in the side and adjusted his position in the seat. "Well, there's the Christmas tree."

"What else?"

"And snow. There's snow."

"You don't need Christmas to have snow."

Winfield turned the heater down. He felt his temper getting away from him again. "There's Christmas dinner. And maybe *you* don't, and maybe *I* don't get any presents, but other people do."

"Maybe you don't *give* any presents, maybe that's why you don't *get* any presents?"

A chill rippled down Winfield's spine. He turned the heater

back up. This twelve-year-old had the soul of a forty-year-old. "People sing carols at Christmas time," said Winfield, trying to hang onto his control. He turned the cruiser onto Temple Road. "How far down is it?"

"My father's not far away now."

Winfield fell silent.

Impatiently, Luke pursued the conversation. "Well, come on, aren't you going to give me anymore Christmas spirit? Aren't you going to give me the old line about families being together? You know . . . about being with the people you love most in the whole world?"

"You're the one that said that." But Winfield's thoughts were on the Christmas his own family—his wife, his son and Gramps—trimmed an eight-foot tree with hand-me-down ornaments Gramps called 'old treasures.'

"Pull over here." Luke directed him to a lonely spot where the long drive was covered with deep snow, too hazardous to negotiate in the cruiser. Opening the door, he said, "House is back in the woods. I'll go it alone from here."

"No, you won't," Winfield said getting out of the car. "I'm going with you to speak to your father."

The child shrugged. "Have it your way."

Winfield took out his Kel-lite, and the two started down the dark, snow-covered drive on foot.

"I don't like your attitude," said Winfield.

"What attitude?"

Winfield nearly choked on the words. "Your negativism."

"That's a heavy duty word. What am I so negative about?"

Winfield began to realize what made him so uncomfortable about this child. "People. Christmas. Your family."

"Was it like that for you when you were a kid?"

Dim memories began to flicker like a candle at the end of a long, dark hallway. They almost hurt. "Yeah. It was like that for me once." With false detachment he looked about at the snow-burdened bushes and tree limbs.

"What do you remember?" asked the child without insolence as he stared up at the policeman plowing through the snow next to him.

"I remember the smell of turkey and pumpkin pie coming from the kitchen. There were only three of us then. Just me, my mother and Gramps. Gramps kept us together after my father . . . committed suicide." His eyes watered, causing him to hesitate before speaking again. "We'd sing carols after dinner. I opened my presents in the morning. They weren't much, as I remember, but they were all Gramps could afford."

"What was your favorite present?" the boy asked gently.

Winfield thought for a moment. "It was a sheriff's badge in the shape of a star. My grandfather made it, but you'll never guess how."

The boy regarded him out of softened eyes. "How?"

"Out of an old tin can lid! I swear!" Winfield laughed in spite of himself. "I haven't thought of that in years! That old fool, sitting there with his tin snips, cutting up old tin cans."

The boy giggled. Infected with the laughter, Winfield caught himself howling and wiped his eyes under pretext of hilarity.

They trudged along in the snow silently for a while until the child finally asked, "You still got that star?"

"I think it's someplace over at my grandfather's." Winfield turned suddenly sober. "Maybe I'll go over there and look for it. Tomorrow afternoon." He cleared his throat, then corrected himself. "Christmas Day. Maybe I can find it."

Just then Winfield heard a soft thud behind them. He spun in a half crouch, making sure the boy was shielded behind him. In an instant his gun was out. His heart thundered in his chest as he searched the snow-covered area with his flashlight beam. To his relief the light revealed a bare branch where a clump of snow had slid to the ground.

Winfield let out a sigh, straightened his posture and holstered his gun. "It's OK, just some snow," he said to the boy, re-checking the area with his flashlight.

Winfield received no answer, so he turned toward the child, but he was gone. "Luke?" he called softly, then more loudly. Still no answer. He realized looking at the ground that there were no tracks leading away from where the child had stood. He turned in the direction of the road, and shining his flashlight on the ground, saw there was only one set of footprints in the snow. They were his.

Christmas and the New Year

Ambrose Bierce

In our manner of observing Christmas there is much, no doubt, that is absurd. Christmas is to some extent a day of meaningless ceremonies, false sentiment and hollow compliments endlessly iterated and misapplied. The observances "appropriate to the day" had, many of them, their origin in an age with which our own has little in common and in countries whose social and religious characteristics were unlike those obtaining here. As in so many other matters, America has in this been content to take her heritage without inquiry and without alteration, sacredly preserving much that once had a meaning now lost, much that is now an anachronism, a mere "survival." Even to the Christmas vocabulary we have added little. St. Nicholas himself, the patron saint of deceived children, still masquerades under the Spanish feminine title of "Santa" and the German nickname of "Claus." The back of our American coal grate is still idealized as a "yule log," and the English "holly" is supposed in most cases fitly to be shadowed forth by a cedar bough, while a comparatively innocuous but equally inedible indigenous comestible figures as the fatal English "plum pudding." Nearly all our Christmas literature is, *longo intervallo,* European in spirit and Dickensish in form. In short, we have Christmas merely because we were in the line of succession. We have taken it as it was transmitted, and we try to make the worst of it.

The approach of the season is apparent in the manner of the friend or relative whose orbs furtively explore your own, seeking

a sign of what you are going to give him; in the irrepressible so-
licitations of babes and cloutlings; in wild cascades of such literature as *Greenleaf on Evidence, for Boys* ("Boot-Leg" series), *The
Little Girls' Illustrated Differential Calculus* and *Aunt Hetty's Ra-
belais,* in words of one syllable. Most clearly is the advent of the
blessed anniversary manifest in maddening iteration of the greeting
wherein, with a precision that never by any chance mistakes its
adjective, you are wished a "merry" Christmas by the same person who a week later will be making ninety-nine "happies" out of
a possible hundred in New Year greetings similarly insincere and
similarly insufferable. It is unknown to me why a Christmas should
be always merry but never happy, and why the happiness appropriate to the New Year should not be expressed in merriment. These
be mysteries in whose penetration abundance of human stupidity
might be disclosed. By the time that one has been wished a "merry
Christmas" or a "happy New Year" some scores of times in the
course of a morning walk, by persons who he knows care nothing about either his merriment or his happiness, he is disposed,
if he is a person of right feeling, to take a pessimist view of the
"compliments of the season" and of the season of compliments.
He cherishes, according to disposition, a bitter animosity or a tol-
erant contempt toward his race. He relinquishes for another year
his hope of meeting some day a brilliant genius or inspired idiot
who will have the intrepidity to vary the adjective and wish him a
"happy Christmas" or a "merry New Year"; or with an even more
captivating originality, keep his mouth shut.

As to the sum of sincerity and genuine good will that utters
itself in making and accepting gifts (the other distinctive feature
of holiday time) statistics, unhappily, are wanting and estimates
untrustworthy. It may reasonably be assumed that the custom,
though largely a survival—gifts having originally been given in
a propitiatory way by the weak to the powerful—is something
more; the present of a goggle-eyed doll from a man six feet high
to a baby twenty-nine inches long not being lucidly explainable
by assumption of an interested motive.

To the children the day is delightful and instructive. It enables them to see their elders in all the various stages of interesting idiocy, and teaches them by means of the Santa Claus deception that exceedingly hard liars may be good mothers and fathers and miscellaneous relatives—thus habituating the infant mind to charitable judgment and establishing an elastic standard of truth that will be useful in their later life.

The annual recurrence of the "carnival of crime" at Christmas has been variously accounted for by different authorities. By some it is supposed to be providential dispensation intended to heighten the holiday joys of those who are fortunate enough to escape with their lives. Others attribute it to the lax morality consequent upon the demand for presents, and still others to the remorse inspired by consciousness of ruinous purchases. It is affirmed by some that persons deliberately and with malice aforethought put themselves in the way of being killed, in order to avert the tiresome iteration of Christmas greetings. If this is correct, the annual Christmas "holocaust" is not an evil demanding abatement, but a blessing to be received in a spirit of devout and pious gratitude.

When the earth in its eternal circumgression arrives at the point where it was at the same time the year before, the sentimentalist whom Christmas has not exhausted of his essence squeezes out his pitiful dreg of emotion to baptize the New Year withal. He dusts and polishes his aspirations, and reërects his resolve, extracting these well-worn properties from the cobwebby corners of his moral lumber-room, whither they were relegated three hundred and sixty-four days before. He "swears off." In short, he sets the centuries at defiance, breaks the sequence of cause and effect, repeals the laws of nature and makes himself a new disposition from a bit of nothing left over at the creation of the universe. He cannot add an inch to his stature, but thinks he can add a virtue to his character. He cannot shed his nails, but believes he can renounce his vices. Unable to eradicate a freckle from his skin, he is confident he can decree a habit out of his conduct. An improvident friend of mine writes upon his mirror with a bit of soap the cabalistic word, AFAHMASP. This is the *fiat lux* to create the shining virtue of thrift, for it means, A Fool And His Money Are Soon Parted. What need have we of morality's countless ministries; the complicated machinery of the church; recurrent suasions of precept and unceasing counsel of example; pursuing din of homily; still, small voice of solicitude and inaudible argument of surroundings — if one may make of himself what he will with a mirror and a bit of soap? But (it may be urged) if one cannot reform himself, how can he reform others? Dear reader, let us have a frank understanding. He cannot.

The practice of inflating the midnight steam-shrieker and belaboring the nocturnal ding-dong to frighten the encroaching New Year is obviously ineffectual, and might profitably be discontinued. It is no whit more sensible and dignified than the custom of savages who beat their sounding dogs to scare away an eclipse. If one elects to live with barbarians, one must endure the barbarous noises of their barbarous superstitions, but the disagreeable simpleton who sits up till midnight to ring a bell or fire a gun because the earth has arrived at a given point in its orbit should nevertheless be deprecated as an enemy to his race. He is a sore trial to the feelings, an affliction almost too sharp for endurance. If he and his sentimental abettors might be melted and cast into a great bell, every right-minded man would derive an innocent delight from pounding it, not only on January first but all the year long.

A Hollow Christmas

Randy McNutt

Carl Rudd first arrived in the timeless hollow, near a small town named Blue Creek, in the late 1960s. The automobile worker was searching for pocketknives to add to his collection, but instead he found another treasure. He bought a 150-year-old converted log house on forty acres on Cassel Run, sent for his wife and ten children in Dayton, and started life anew in rugged Adams County. Local people, usually shy and taciturn around strangers, accepted Carl right away. He was friendly and natural, and he shared with them his peculiar dream.

He wanted to build one of the nation's larger private Christmas displays right there in the hollow. Never mind that it was in the middle of nowhere, or that the one-lane gravel road was barely accessible, or that he refused to charge admission, or that there were no parking lots. He just felt that this was the right time and place. As neighbor Truman Boldman recalled, "Pretty soon after he started the display, he came over to my house and he said, 'Looks like I 'bout took over your place, too.' I just said, 'I don't care what you do.' Old Carl is a good guy. Everybody in the holler likes him."

I first met him in the 1970s when I was an inexperienced young reporter for a Cincinnati newspaper. When the Associated Press sent my first story on Rudd's Christmas Farm to newspapers across the nation, Carl thought I was a genuine ink-stained magician. I explained that such coverage came purely by chance, but he just smiled knowingly.

Becoming further intrigued by his light farm, I asked more questions and wrote more stories for national publications. Carl and I became friends. Although we had little in common, we connected in an inexplicable way. He was easy to talk to, and he would call me at the office every December 24. "Have a *joyous* Christmas, my friend," he would say in his friendly way, and I would feel warm inside. The man really meant it. As soon as I heard his voice, my spirits brightened. Carl exuded a faith and happiness that he could not conceal. To thousands of people, he meant Christmas in Appalachian Ohio.

But he did not make people happy on faith alone. It took a lot of physical exertion. On steamy August days in the early 1980s, Carl started preparing for Christmas. He dragged several eight-foot candles—the ones cities use to decorate their downtown streets—from his barn and cleaned them. He and his children lugged five-hundred-pound plaster angels up the steep hillsides. (They're called hills in Blue Creek, but they look like small mountains to this city man.) Before the October chill could turn to November cold, he had strung lights across the hills and nine-foot angels from hardy sycamores by the creek. Tinsel-covered archways led up into the woods, where paths had been cut through the timberland. "One night a long time ago," Boldman recalled, "I looked up and saw all them lights come on, and then the cars commenced to rollin' down our little road and—whew! Then come busloads of people. You can get into quite a jam up here if you don't watch out. Before old Carl moved here, you could lay down in the road for an hour and not get hit. Now, the traffic is backed up all the way down to the old iron bridge."

Over the years, Carl added twenty-five thousand feet of concrete pathways and steps so that the physically disabled could visit the display, and an additional ten thousand lights—to make an estimated one million. "Give or take a few thousand," he said, chuckling. While installing the steps, he was nearly bitten by a copperhead. He pulled and strained many muscles while lugging his heavy figures up into the hills.

As the display's fame grew in the late 1980s, county officials blacktopped and widened the small road and featured the display in local tourism guides. The Blue Creek post office also started canceling mail with a stamp of Rudd's Christmas Farm. Gradually, the farm became at least a little more accessible, although motorists continued to drive over several rickety wooden bridges that were no more than slats lying across creeks. Yet visitors kept coming from as far away as Michigan, Illinois, and Pennsylvania. In the late 1980s, Carl decided to make the display permanent because it was too difficult to dismantle every January. "I've carried sheep down these hills until I don't want to look at another one again," he once told me. "And them angels, well, you don't want to lift one 'cause it'll nearly kill you. Takes three men and a boy just to lift one. Thankfully, the camels stay in place all year."

The selling of Christmas, although it sounds trite to even say it, is the reason for his display. "People have their minds on everything but the real thing," he said. "We're not in this for the money, only to show the real meaning of Christmas. We want to tell the story of Christ. We're not artists or nothing. We cut those signs over there out of simple plywood and decorated them with Bible verses. We got eight acres of plywood shepherds, nativity scenes, live donkeys—you name it. It does cost a lot to light this place, but the Lord always provides a way. I'm just about the poorest in Adams County, but I'm the happiest."

On a cold afternoon a few years later, Carl escorted me into the house to see his wife Judy. Their warmth and affection made me feel good, as though I had known them all my life. The telephone rang. Another "customer."

"Hello," Carl said softly.

"Is this the Christmas man?"

"That's me."

"Is your farm open tonight, being Christmas Eve and all?"

"Un-huh. Sure is."

"With lights and all?"

"They'll be on from five thirty to ten thirty of an ev'nin'. Bless you."

Carl hung up the phone and told us, "I had a guy come in from Louisville, and he almost got mad when I wouldn't turn the lights on. I finally had to do it to keep him happy. But I have to be careful when I do it, see, 'cause as soon as I turn 'em on, they attract people from all over the countryside. Oh, well, what's it gonna hurt to turn 'em on a little early if somebody's come so far?"

"It hurts the wallet," Judy said with a smile.

"Honey," Carl said, "that's all there is to life, giving people happiness. What else is there? You can't take anything with you, can you?"

He walked into the front room of his old house and felt the frigid air infiltrating the log walls. He bent down and checked a potbellied stove that heated the room. Warm air flowed through its iron grill. On a table beside him, a set of golden bells played a melody as they lighted up one by one. He grinned happily.

Christmas lights always did fascinate Carl. For three decades he continued to acquire them from individuals, cities, and small towns. When people asked him why, he said, "I just buy 'em. I'm a pack rat." Then he'd laugh. "We went up to Franklin, Michigan—that's the name of the place, ain't it Mother?—for a big light show. They didn't have nothin' like I do. Now, I'm not braggin', you see. I mean, I started decoratin' my house in Dayton in the early sixties, and we'd draw twenty thousand—in one season. Then I bought a display from Ford and another from the city of Loveland a few years ago. I waited a long time for the Loveland sale to come up."

His Christmas arsenal included 150 sheep figures, 9 five-hundred-pound angels, a snowmaker, dozens of life-size shepherds, 6 big camels, dozens of caroler figures, and thousands of other pieces that he scattered across twenty acres. A tour lasted about thirty minutes and began with a walk up 125 concrete steps that Carl and Judy had built into the hillside.

Eventually, they tamed the farmland that once yielded crops. Carl erected a large nativity scene and a light-studded star of Bethlehem at the top of the hill. He also installed wiring and huge speakers that he controlled from a switch on his front porch. Gospel Christmas music floated among the trees and down to the narrow road, echoing into the woods.

"The idea for a Christmas display came from my childhood during the Depression in Kentucky," Carl explained. "On many nights we hardly had anything to eat, but we got by. I used to look up at the stars and say, 'Lord, if I ever have the opportunity to tell the world about you, I surely will. I will tell the story of your birth. And I will always make you as free as the air I breathe.' That's why I don't charge to see the display. Judy and me have had to go to banks and loan companies to borrow money. But the good Lord always helped us pay the bills."

She said, "We believe that people need something to pick them up."

As Carl and I walked up the big hill next to his house, I started feeling slightly winded. Carl moved briskly, despite multiple open-heart surgeries. At the summit, he announced, "If visitors come to see Santa Claus, they've come to the wrong place. My goal is to depict the life of Christ from birth to death. I'd say 150,000 people came through here last year—a million folks over the years. Makes me wonder how they all got here. We had to make a trail with sixteen tons of gravel so they could walk in these hills. We gave out fifteen hundred pounds of candy. People come here to get away from everything. I see people in the city shopping centers and they're lookin' so angry, but not out here. They see this simple display by a guy who can't read or write, a guy with a third-grade education, and they smile. In all the years, I've never had one thing stolen or one person say he was disappointed. I guess I've spent a lot of money over time—heck, I never did keep track. I feel this is where I need to be. It makes me happy." He pointed to the road, as if imagining cars lining up. "A lot of people can't understand me," he went on. "All I want to give is happiness." His eyes locked onto his house, where "Rudd Christmas Farm" was spelled out in red lights. "That one's for the airplanes," Carl said, laughing.

Even when viewed from the top of the hill, his display looked massive: one man's tribute to the real Christmas. By the late 1990s, an average of two hundred thousand people — by Carl's estimate — were coming annually from Thanksgiving to New Year's Day. Major news organizations continued to tell the farm's story. He never charged admission, but in those later years he did reluctantly accept donations to help pay his large electricity bills. He realized that if he didn't receive some help, he might have to cut back. He knew that was not an option. "It is my whole life," he said of the display. "I've been putting up the lights for so long, I can't remember not doing it."

And he smiled.

One million lights. Two million visitors. A multitude of joy.

That was the tally after a lifetime of enlightenment.

When I visited Carl in December of 2003, at the start of the display's final season, he seemed enthusiastic. In his early seventies by then, Carl suffered from cancer and Alzheimer's disease, and could no longer tend to the massive display. "All this is breaking my heart," he said. "I have built up this farm to tell the Christmas story. So it's hard for me to tear it down and walk away. When I came to Adams County thirty years ago, not one neighbor complained about the lights and the cars. The Lord took an old man and used him to send the message all over the world. I've walked around this farm with reporters from NBC, ABC, CBS — even *The New York Times*. They watched me string lights across the trees and hills and flip on twelve hundred amps. When I first started, I flipped the switch and burned up the big electric company feeder line. The superintendent called and said, 'Carl, buddy, take it easy. Turn 'em on one set at a time.' We haven't had a power failure in years."

As Judy headed to the kitchen to bake cookies for visitors, Carl walked out front to set up large wooden Christmas figures one more time. Nothing had changed with the farm's rustic decor and hand-lettered signs. When the wind blew, chimes rang throughout the trees and everything gently shook — big candy canes, wise men, carolers, angels, and wreaths. I looked up in a tree and noticed a large surrealistic angel made of gold tinsel holding a trumpet next to its face—a slightly-too-small doll's head. Across the woods rung familiar melodies—"Away in a Manager" and "The Old Rugged Cross." In the gray cloudy afternoon, the farm looked rough-hewn and incongruent, but still honest.

"I can walk through these hills and hear people talking," he told me. "The children say, 'Mom, what does this scene say?' I love that. I remember one time when we had a busload of blind people come though here. They got to talking, and it really got to me. I wondered how they could appreciate the place. But they said they 'saw' by hearing the people talking through the hills.

"Now, this ain't to say we haven't had it rough at times ourselves. Judy has had twenty-five surgeries; I've had a total of fourteen now. But we were just thankful to show people love. I always said, 'Lord, please don't let me get that Alzheimer's.' But for some reason, he has seen fit for me to get the disease. I know he has a plan, though. I'm taking chelation therapy, an alternative medicine treatment that cleanses the blood of metallic impurities. It has helped me tremendously. Some time ago I could barely remember my own name. Now I can—and I can work outdoors again. I know I'm all right when I get to thinking about how wonderful it is to know Jesus."

In the gray afternoon light, we looked down on the peaceful world that Carl Rudd knew and loved. Neither one of us spoke.

"Won't you come and stay with us awhile?" he asked.

Judy welcomed us at the door. Carl told her that he was feeling so good that he might put up some decorations next year.

"Carl," she said, gently, "maybe thirty-six years is enough." She smiled.

He picked up an auctioneer's list, which featured pieces of his world that would be sold next month. What a way to kick off a new year. We all sat down at the kitchen table, and he began reading aloud from the list: "Christmas display decorations: eight angels, eight and a half feet tall, from Greece, 1930s; four small plastic angels, thirty-three inches tall; nineteen angels, thirty inches tall; two kneeling angels, life size; two heralding angels, six feet; five wrought iron angels; eleven animated angels; one angel, three feet; twenty twelve-inch poinsettias; twenty-two seven-inch single candles; twelve six-foot lamp posts; forty plastic candy canes; eight six-foot double candles; ten stars, six and a half feet each; twenty-three eight-foot hanging trees; sixty-nine lanterns. . . ."

His voice grew softer, trailing off.

Judy said, "Carl, we understand." She touched his hand.

He continued: " . . . nineteen sheep; lamb; eleven shepherds; standing wise man; three wise men on camels; manger scene with Mary, Joseph, Baby, and crib, sheep dog, ram, lying sheep, donkey, cow, two small donkeys, three calves; Seasons Greetings sign; two forty-foot Merry Christmas signs; Bethlehem star and streamers; six large wreaths with candles; three large yellow trees; two candelabra stands; five animated dolls; ceramic choir; five wrought iron palm trees. . . ."

Carl pushed the sheet in front of me. In my mind I continued to read the lifetime of collecting: "large grapevine wreath; three bells; train; church and choir; angel in empty tomb; two cement angels; five large plastic candles; Jesus and Disciples; Jesus and blind man; Jesus and woman at the well; seventeen religious paintings; fifteen small aluminum trees; lots of tinsel; eleven green painted trees; strobe lighting on crosses; archways; small red house with Christmas display; steel touring sled with three seats."

Carl broke an uncomfortable silence: "I can't get used to the thought of sitting around at Christmas." He tried to laugh. "I'm tenderhearted when I think of the things we used to do here. I want the Lord to help me remember better so that I won't forget the faces of all the wonderful friends I've known. I keep hopin', too. Maybe next year we can do it again."

Again, the silence hurt.

<hr>

On a recent Christmas Eve, the hollow is gray and quiet. Only the wind moves along Cassel Run Road. I drive slowly and peer westward, toward his little house. But I see no lights, no angels. I hear no music. The only sounds I hear are the whistling breeze and the cries of a gray tomcat that wants his supper. I want to leave, but somehow I can't. While on assignment in the area I had decided to drive over to see Carl's place, and see it I must. So I step out of the car and leave the door wide open. I stare—at his house, then toward the fading afternoon sun.

Without the display to tame it, the hollow reverts to its origins. It is a willful paradise, choreographed by the Almighty Himself. I pause momentarily to watch it unfold. The panorama changes before my eyes: A light fog cloaks an orange sun and a tree-filled world bleached by frost. Finally the sun pokes through, faintly illuminating a lopsided barn that looks like a paper silhouette against a small patch of rosy sky. A cloudy sundown will lead me on my drive back to the city.

For another moment I stand there pondering why the hollow once attracted visitors from far beyond these simple hills. I'm certain that the sheer *quantity* of lights had much to do with it, but I know there was more—something I cannot understand. Perhaps the farm's unashamed simplicity touched people's souls as well as their eyes. For many of them, Carl's work, so heartfelt and ministerial, shone through the woods as brightly as his lights.

By now I feel a nagging sadness that only the ghosts of Christmas past can summon. My mother always made the holiday special. I miss her, my father, and our family gatherings on Christmas Eves so long ago. I wonder what Carl's adopted families—thousands of them—will be doing on this night, their first Eve without him. They will neither taste his cookies nor feel his warm handshake. Now Rudd's Christmas Farm is history—another faded tradition.

A cold wind blows against my collar. I see only skeletons of trees and dark shadows filling up Rudd's Christmas Farm. Not one car is in sight. As I pull away from the little white house, I can hear still Carl Rudd's voice ringing in my mind like a peaceful bell: "You never know what the Good Lord has in store. He has a plan for us all. Have a *joyous* Christmas, my friend."

Ben

Kay Boyle

Ben was a black man who pushed rolling chairs on the boardwalk once, but before the war even he wanted to belong to Puss, and in 1917 he gave himself to Puss forever. Puss was my little grandfather, and he bought Ben a dark-green jacket with dull buttons on it, and three alpaca aprons so that he could change often and keep looking smart. He learned how to wait at table and do the shoes and tend the furnace and use the vacuum cleaner. He was so big he had to stoop as he passed under every doorway in the house; he stooped down from his height and stooped in reverence as he took the little white man's orders. He could have stood Puss up on the palm of his hand and snapped him in two like a white-headed weed, but his voice instead was hushed with awe when he spoke to the saucy little man. All the time he harked to what Puss said, his head hung low and his full slack heavy lip hung down, in shame for his height and in shame for his strength and for having gone bald too soon.

Every room in the place became theirs in a while, theirs to go into, the four flights up and down. Through the furnace room and the cellar where the shower baths stood with bathing suits and old caps hanging in them, past the laundry and up the stairs into the library and the dining room. Through the halls and in and out of the conservatory they went on their journeys of perquisition: the little white man first in his silk skullcap and his doeskin slippers, and the black man big as a giant in his jacket and apron following behind. Through the pantry, the kitchen, and up the back way to the bathrooms they went, picking up, collecting.

"Here, just catch hold of that, Ben," Puss said, and the black man answered:

"Yes suh, yes suh, I got it right heah in my apron."

Into the guests' rooms and the bedrooms after the friends and family had left them, their marvelous excursions into tidiness took place. Here they redeemed a glove without its mate dropped on the top of a bookcase, here the top of a fountain pen, and somewhere else a postcard from the Poconos. Stray toothbrushes, balls of wool, schoolbooks, odd knitting needles, bracelets or rings removed to wash the hands and forgotten next to the soap, all these lay within their province of impeccability.

"Here, just pick that up, Ben," my little grandfather said, and Ben answered:

"Yes suh, yes suh, I got it right heah, suh."

Any time of day you could go up to Puss's door and knock, and he cleared his throat before pronouncing distinctly:

"Come in." And when he saw it was a child he added: "Come in, come in, whoever you are! Come in!"

Inside, his room was furnished like a business executive's: a glass-topped desk, a swivel chair, and standing alphabetic files. On the desk stood a green glass-shaped chromium office lamp, and there were two wire wastepaper baskets placed on either side of his chair with never more than a single slightly crumpled sheet of paper dropped in the bottom of one. His room was at the top of the house and through its windows you could see the roofs of the other Atlantic City houses and the vast sea moving quietly beyond.

You could say, "Puss, I've lost a doll's shoe," and he pinched his glasses on his nose and reached out for the card file and slid the box to him across the desk. His well-manicured, small fingers ran rapidly through the alphabet to "S," through the long list of variously described scissors they had retrieved to "Shaving: one brush (boar's hair), 6 Gillette blades," down to "Shoes," and paused there.

"Shoes," he read out, clearing his throat. "Gumshoes, Kate's silver slippers (tarnished), Madge's low button shoes, one bathing shoe (dark-blue canvas, cord sole), doll's black patent leather with instep strap (one)."

He looked up over his spectacles in inquiry, and if you said yes, that was the one, he rang the electric bell under his desk and Ben came up, coming carefully up the stairs and through the hall and into Puss's room, tiptoeing gingerly as if fearful of disturbing someone's sleep or merely of colliding with the diminutiveness of what was ceiling and wall and house itself around him.

"Number 3 ab, left," Puss said briefly to him, and Ben replied in awe:

"Yes suh, numbah 3 ab, left, suh," and higher even than this fourth floor he went, mounting the final ladder to the attic, his monstrous crouching body carried upwards on his hands and knees.

The attic was kept as clean as wax and stacked neatly with uniform cardboard boxes, for this was how their work went on. All the long winter afternoons, Ben crept across the boards there, too big to stand, sorting and labeling their spoils and closing them away in boxes, while Puss sat at his elegant glass-topped desk below and filled in the lined white file cards with explanation.

"One chile's mitten, suh," Ben would call down through the opening of the trap door in the attic floor, and Puss repeated:

"One child's mitten. Put it in Number 6 fg, right, Ben. What color?"

Ben would wait a minute before he said:

"I cain't tell you that, suh. I couldn't say. I never got to know much about color. I never got that far in school."

I remember Ben, and I remember that year on Christmas morning he came upstairs from stoking the furnace. It was only half-past five, but he saw the light in the hallway from below; and because he had been listening for us he heard us open our doors, and heard us whispering together. Our stockings were filled and pinned up on the velvet hangings where we'd hung them empty the night before. It was while we were unfastening them and holding them crackling wondrously against us that Ben came tiptoeing up the stairs.

"I hung up my stocking too," he whispered across the hall to us. "I sure did. You wait a minute and you'll see."

His mouth was hanging wide open with his joy, and all his teeth showed pure as milk within its cavern. He was dressed already in his jacket and his apron, or maybe it was the way Aunt Madge said, that he never cared about taking his things off at all. Just set the two long human faces of his shoes beside the bed, and laid his green jacket over the chair's back and slept.

"I didn't ask nobody nothing," he said, his voice shaking in his throat with bliss for what would come. "I just hung my stocking up the way you children was doing."

It was lost in the velvet folds of the curtain until he went over and carefully moved the hangings aside, and then we all saw it: the long dark gray woman's stocking with a white seam at the heel, quite new and dangling without life or promise in it. He had hung it up in the dark between where ours had been, but it was empty still because nobody had seen it there.

"I hung up my stocking—" he began, and standing there with his back to us, he lifted one big hand and passed the inside of it over his forehead and the bald part of his head. "I sure hung up my stocking," not understanding and perhaps never getting any nearer to understanding.

We children stood in the lighted hall, holding the still untouched new dolls and the trumpets and the tissue-paper bundles in our arms, and Ben turned slowly around and looked at us in bewilderment. After what seemed a long time, his lips opened and they made no sound, but then he began crying. He did not try to turn his head away, or touch the tears, but let them run unheeded down his face. There was nothing we dared say to him or do, but in a minute we heard a door above us open, and Puss in his doeskin slippers and dressing gown came stepping quickly down the stairs.

"What's this, what's this?" he said, with his white mustaches bristling. "What's up? What's up? Ben, why are you making a spectacle of yourself like this before the children?"

His look darted around the hallway at us, and when he saw

what it was he put his hands into the pockets of his dressing gown and said:

"Now, Ben, I'm very much surprised to see you acting like this. Here you are, a man of thirty, crying like a child!"

"Children ain't got no cause to cry," Ben said, and the tears ran down his face still while he looked at the stockings we held. "I wouldn't be crying if I was a chile today," he said.

"What would your father and mother say if they saw you cutting up like this on Christmas morning?" said Puss. He stood with his hands in his pockets, looking boldly and saucily up the black man's height to where the face hung shining with tears. "A great big fellow like you, over six feet tall and strong enough to carry the whole house around on your shoulders! Why, I'm ashamed of you!"

I remember Ben, and how he wiped his hand across his face, drawing the side of it under his wide-nostriled, seemingly boneless nose.

"That old Santa," he began, and Puss interrupted him, moving his hands a little uncomfortably in the pockets of his gown.

"Come, come, Ben," he said. "This is no way to talk. Perhaps your Christmas is coming later. Perhaps old Santy—"

"That's my Christmas," said Ben before he went tiptoeing down the stairs, his shoulders stooped in pain. "There's my Christmas hanging up, still waiting—" And we turned and looked again, holding our toys against us, at the long gray empty cotton stocking that nobody had ever worn.

I remember him, and how he used to make the fire in the living room in the evenings, crossing the fur rug on his hands and knees and reaching the big logs in. The place was dark, and when he put the match to the kindling, the flame ran fast along the edge of the paper. Kneeling like this, he took the combs out of his pocket one evening and opened the tissue paper they lay in and showed me what they were. I was sitting up in the armchair, looking, and the fire's reflection streamed bright as oil across his forehead and flanged his nostrils and his naked throat with light.

"I got the ones with the jewels in them because they was the best," he said. They were the kind of tortoise-shell combs a lady wears in her hair, and these had stones set in them: turquoise, and pearl, and some sort of cut pinkish jewels that sparkled as beautifully as glass. "I got to have the best now for everybody I got anything to do with and no mistake about it," he said. "Your grandfather, I learned a lot from him I never thought of knowing. About having a home," he said, "and keeping things neat and right just like anybody ought to. I didn't pick these out just nohow. I kept in mind the different dresses she'd be wearing. They're for my wife," he said without looking up. "They're for my wife," he said, kneeling there and holding them tenderly in the paper.

"When did you get married, Ben?" I asked him, whispering as he did across the darkness. "I never knew you had a wife. I didn't know."

"I got her all picked out," he said. He folded the tissue paper over the combs, his fingers long and broad, and hairless as a savage's would be. "I saw her on the boardwalk once, but I ain't going to be hurried into nothing. I ain't going to be rushed into nothing by nobody," he said. "I'm biding my time for this year, anyway. I'm going to do my courting easy and slow."

That was the year before he died of the Spanish influenza, and after it Puss made his excursions into immaculateness from the cellar up to the foot of the attic's ladder alone. One day in the laundry, behind the bars of washing soap, wrapped in tissue paper still and tied with a tinsel ribbon that had "Yuletide Greetings, Yuletide Greetings, Yuletide Greetings" stamped the length of it in red, Puss found the side combs for a lady's hair. In the afternoon, he sat down at his glass-topped desk and made out their card in the box file for them: "Two celluloid hair combs, new, ornamented with jewels (imitation)." Later he climbed the ladder to the attic, going slowly in his doeskin slippers and wearing his black skullcap, and he put them away in a box labeled with some number or another and slipped it into its place either to the left or right of the trap door.

A Visit from St. Nicholas

IN THE ERNEST HEMINGWAY MANNER

James Thurber

It was the night before Christmas. The house was very quiet. No creatures were stirring in the house. There weren't even any mice stirring. The stockings had been hung carefully by the chimney. The children hoped that Saint Nicholas would come and fill them.

The children were in their beds. Their beds were in the room next to ours. Mamma and I were in our beds. Mamma wore a kerchief. I had my cap on. I could hear the children moving. We didn't move. We wanted the children to think we were asleep.

"Father," the children said.

There was no answer. He's there, all right, they thought.

"Father," they said, and banged on their beds.

"What do you want?" I asked.

"We have visions of sugarplums," the children said.

"Go to sleep," said mamma.

"We can't sleep," said the children. They stopped talking, but I could hear them moving. They made sounds.

"Can you sleep?" asked the children.

"No," I said.

"You ought to sleep."

"I know. I ought to sleep."

"Can we have some sugarplums?"

"You can't have any sugarplums," said mamma.

"We just asked you."

There was a long silence. I could hear the children moving again.

"Is Saint Nicholas asleep?" asked the children.

"No," mamma said. "Be quiet."

"What the hell would he be asleep tonight for?" I asked.

"He might be," the children said.

"He isn't," I said.

"Let's try to sleep," said mamma.

The house became quiet once more. I could hear the rustling noises the children made when they moved in their beds.

Out on the lawn a clatter arose. I got out of bed and went to the window. I opened the shutters; then I threw up the sash. The moon shone on the snow. The moon gave the lustre of mid-day to objects in the snow. There was a miniature sleigh in the snow, and eight tiny reindeer. A little man was driving them. He was lively and quick. He whistled and shouted at the reindeer and called them by their names. Their names were Dasher, Dancer, Prancer, Vixen, Comet, Cupid, Donder, and Blitzen.

He told them to dash away to the top of the porch, and then he told them to dash away to the top of the wall. They did. The sleigh was full of toys.

"Who is it?" mamma asked.

"Some guy," I said. "A little guy."

I pulled my head in out of the window and listened. I heard the reindeer on the roof. I could hear their hoofs pawing and prancing on the roof.

"Shut the window," said mamma.

I stood still and listened.

"What do you hear?"

"Reindeer," I said. I shut the window and walked about. It was cold. Mamma sat up in the bed and looked at me.

"How would they get on the roof?" mamma asked.

"They fly."

"Get into bed. You'll catch cold."

Mamma lay down in bed. I didn't get into bed. I kept walking around.

"What do you mean, they fly?" asked mamma.

"Just fly is all."

Mamma turned away toward the wall. She didn't say anything.

I went out into the room where the chimney was. The little man came down the chimney and stepped into the room. He was dressed all in fur. His clothes were covered with ashes and soot from the chimney. On his back was a pack like a peddler's pack. There were toys in it. His cheeks and nose were red and he had dimples. His eyes twinkled. His mouth was little, like a bow, and his beard was very white. Between his teeth was a stumpy pipe. The smoke from the pipe encircled his head in a wreath. He laughed and his belly shook. It shook like a bowl of red jelly. I laughed. He winked his eye, then he gave a twist to his head. He didn't say anything.

He turned to the chimney and filled the stockings and turned away from the chimney. Laying his finger aside his nose, he gave a nod. Then he went up the chimney. I went to the chimney and looked up. I saw him get into his sleigh. He whistled at his team and the team flew away. The team flew as lightly as thistledown. The driver called out, "Merry Christmas and good night." I went back to bed.

"What was it?" asked mamma. "Saint Nicholas?" She smiled.

"Yeah," I said.

She sighed and turned in the bed.

"I saw him," I said.

"Sure."

"I did see him."

"Sure you saw him." She turned farther toward the wall.

"Father," said the children.

"There you go," mamma said. "You and your flying reindeer."

"Go to sleep," I said.

"Can we see Saint Nicholas when he comes?" the children asked.

"You got to be asleep," I said. "You got to be asleep when he comes. You can't see him unless you're unconscious."

"Father knows," mamma said.

I pulled the covers over my mouth. It was warm under the covers. As I went to sleep I wondered if mamma was right.

Contributors

RANE ARROYO is the author of ten books of poems, a collection of short stories, and selected plays. From Chicago, he is a gay Puerto Rican thriving in Toledo, Ohio. Though he has wandered across the planet, he finds the Midwest to be his home and his heart.

AMBROSE BIERCE was born in 1842 in Horse Cave Creek, a commune in Meigs County, Ohio, where he lived until the age of four, at which time his family relocated to Indiana. As a teenager, he returned to Ohio, living with his uncle Lucius in Akron. The seminal event in his life was service in the 9th Indiana Infantry during the American Civil War. His engagements at Shiloh, Pickett's Mill, and Chickamauga resulted in the subject matter that would define his writing career. Among his revered works are *The Fiend's Delight, Cobwebs from an Empty Skull, The Devil's Dictionary,* and *Tales of Soldiers and Civilians,* which contains his most famous story, "Occurrence at Owl Creek Bridge." Following his final publication in 1913, he disappeared mysteriously without a trace.

KAY BOYLE (1902–1992) grew up in Cincinnati, Ohio, where she studied music and the arts before relocating to France at the age of twenty-one. She became part of the community of ex-patriots living and working in Europe in the years between the wars. She was forced by the outbreak of WWII to return to America where she participated in campaigns against fascism and in favor of women's rights. A prolific author, she published ten novels, numerous collections of short stories, and other writings. Her most famous works include *Short Stories* (1929), *My Next Bride* (1934), and *Death of a Man* (1936), which drew attention to the atrocities of Nazism.

PAUL LAURENCE DUNBAR (1872–1906) was the first African American poet to attain national prominence. He was born in Dayton, Ohio, the son of former slaves; his father escaped his bonds and served during the American Civil War as a soldier in the 55th Massachusetts Infantry Regiment. Inspired by his mother's love of poetry, Dunbar began writing verse at the age of six. His first volume, *Oak and Ivy,* attracted modest attention, but his second book, *Majors and Minors,* propelled him into the national consciousness. During his short thirty-three years, he produced twelve books of poetry, four collections of short fiction, and five novels.

SCOTT GEISEL has published stories in a variety of journals and anthologies. He was a finalist for the 2008 Eric Hoffer Award for fiction and has a story included in *Best New Writing 2008.* He was a founding coeditor of *MudRock: Stories and Tales* and an assistant editor for both *Flash Fiction Forward* and *New Sudden Fiction.* In conjunction with the Dayton Metro Library, Geisel established a series of teen writing workshops and a publication. He is creator and editor of *Gravity Fiction,* short stories by college writers, and he teaches at Wright State University.

NIKKI GIOVANNI, though born in Tennessee, grew up in Lincoln Heights, a suburb of Cincinnati, Ohio. Following the publication of her first book of poetry, *Black Feeling Black Talk* in 1968, she initiated a career in letters that resulted in Oprah Winfrey proclaiming her one of twenty-five "Living Legends." An honoree and selection for the Ohio Women's Hall of Fame, Giovanni continues to produce best-selling volumes of poetry. She is the author of thirty books and is a Distinguished Professor at Virginia Tech University.

WILLIAM DEAN HOWELLS (1837–1920) was born in what is now Martins Ferry, Ohio, the son of a printer and publisher, an auspicious beginning for a writer. Following service to the Lincoln presidential campaign, he was appointed U.S. Consul to Venice where he lived for four years. Upon his return to America, he secured the position of editor of *The Atlantic Monthly,* where he became a proponent of realism and assisted in the emerging careers of Mark Twain, Henry James, and Paul Laurence Dunbar. Hailed as "the Dean of American Letters," he published over one hundred volumes of fiction, poetry, nonfiction, and criticism. His most revered book is his 1885 novel, *The Rise of Silas Lapham.*

LANGSTON HUGHES (1902–1967), born in Joplin, Missouri, grew up in Cleveland, Ohio, and attended high school there, where he began writing poetry. At twenty-one, he traveled to Africa. Upon his return, he settled in Harlem, becoming a central figure in the Harlem Renaissance during the 1920s. He wrote prolifically up until his death from cancer. Among his works are volumes of poetry, novels, plays, autobiographies, nonfiction, and edited anthologies. The area in Harlem where he lived has been preserved by the City of New York and renamed "Langston Hughes Place."

WENDELL MAYO is author of two story collections, *Centaur of the North* and *B. Horror and Other Stories,* as well as a novel-in-stories, *In Lithuanian Wood.* Over eighty of his short stories have appeared in magazines and anthologies, including the *Yale Review, Harvard Review, Missouri Review, Threepenny Review, Indiana Review,* and *Chicago Review.* Recent work of his has appeared in *Crab Orchard Review, Florida Review,* and *Hawaii Pacific Review.* He is a recipient of a National Endowment for the Arts Creative Writing Fellowship and a Fulbright to Lithuania. Mayo teaches at Bowling Green State University.

RANDY MCNUTT, a native of Hamilton, Ohio, began his writing career as a newspaper and magazine journalist. He has taught writing at Miami University and the University of Cincinnati. He is the author of fourteen books, including *Guitar Towns: A Journey to the Crossroads of Rock'n'Roll* (2002) and *Lost Ohio: More Travels into Haunted Landscapes, Ghost Towns, and For-*

gotten Lives (2006). He lives in Hamilton with his wife, the writer Cheryl Bauer, and their three cats.

ROBERT MILTNER is associate professor of English at Kent State University Stark where he teaches literature and creative writing. He teaches poetry in the Northeast Ohio MFA Consortium in Creative Writing at Kent State University. He is coeditor with Sandra Lee Kleppe of the University of Tromsø, Norway, of the *New Paths to Raymond Carver: Essays on His Life, Fiction, and Poetry*. He is founding editor for *The Raymond Carver Review* and is an officer for the International Raymond Carver Society. Currently, he is editing an anthology of poems about childhood in Ohio. Miltner is the author of chapbooks and artists' collaborative books, including *Rock the Boat, Canyons of Sleep, On the Off Ramp, Box of Light, Fellow Traveler, Ghost of a Chance, Imperative,* and *Against the Simple* (a Wick chapbook award winner). His stories and short fictions have appeared in *Apple Valley Review, Hamilton Stone Review, Rockford Review, Storyglossia,* and *Istanbul Literary Review.* He is at work on a novel, *Tempest.* Miltner has lived most of his life in Ohio, residing variously in Avon Lake, Canton, Cincinnati, and Steubenville, cities mostly along its Great Lake and the Ohio River.

DOROTHY DODGE ROBBINS is associate professor of English at Louisiana Tech University. Her essays and reviews have been published in *The Centennial Review, Critique, Ecumenica, The Midwest Quarterly, Names: A Journal of Onomastics, The Southern Quarterly,* and *The Texas Review.* In collaboration with husband and colleague, Ken Robbins, she coedited *Christmas Stories from Louisiana* (2003), *Christmas on the Great Plains* (2004), and *Christmas Stories from Georgia* (2005). Her roots to the Buckeye State extend back through her parents, John Warren Dodge and Mary Lou (née Fuller) Dodge, who received their degrees from and fell in love at Marietta College, Marietta, Ohio.

KENNETH ROBBINS serves as the director, School of the Performing Arts, Louisiana Tech University. His stories have appeared in

The Briar Cliff Review, Heritage of the Great Plains, The North Dakota Quarterly, St. Andrews Review, The McNeese Review, and *The Southern Quarterly.* His novel, *Buttermilk Bottoms* (University of Iowa Press, 1987), received the Toni Morrison Prize for Fiction and the Associated Writing Programs Novel Award. His plays have been performed in the United States, Canada, Denmark, Ireland, and Japan.

HARRIET BEECHER STOWE (1811–1893), born in Litchfield, Connecticut, moved to Cincinnati at the age of twenty-one when her father received an appointment to serve the Lane Theological Seminary. There she met and married another member of the faculty, Calvin Stowe. At the seminary, she was introduced to the horrors of slavery; she heard stories directly from runaway slaves escaping bondage via the Underground Railroad. Eventually these experiences found their way into her world-renowned novel, *Uncle Tom's Cabin.* In all, she wrote thirty books before her death in Hartford, Connecticut.

JAMES THURBER (1894–1961), one of America's most celebrated humorists, was born in Columbus. He attended Ohio State University but did no complete his degree due to blindness in one eye. An author of nearly forty books of stories, essays, and works for children, he began his writing career as an editor at *The New Yorker.* He received a Tony Award for his Broadway hit, *A Thurber Carnival.* The Thurber House, devoted to his life and heritage, is a living museum located in Columbus.

Sisters JANE ANN TURZILLO and MARY A. TURZILLO used to pass the time waiting for the turkey to roast on Thanksgiving Day by writing a collaborative Christmas story. Each would write until she was tired and then the other would take up the narrative thread. Winner of multiple Ohio Press Women awards, Jane has authored two historical books for Arcadia Publishing. She has published articles and short stories in periodicals across the United States and Canada. Jane holds degrees in Criminal Justice and Mass Media

Communication, and this story reflects her experience as a police reporter. Mary A. Turzillo won a Nebula for her story "Mars Is No Place for Children." She is emeritus professor of English at Kent State University Trumbull Campus. Her first novel, *An Old-Fashioned Martian Girl,* was serialized in *Analog.* Her work has appeared in anthologies and periodicals in the United States, Great Britain, Germany, Italy, the Czech Republic, and Japan.

JULIA DUFFY WARD has published a memoir in *House Beautiful* and travel essays in *The New York Times, New Choices,* and *Travelers' Tales.* Since leaving the Valley, she has lived in eight countries and traveled on five continents. At present Ward lives with her husband in Oxford, Ohio, where she teaches English as a second language at Miami University.

ERIC WASSERMAN is assistant professor of English at the University of Akron where he also teaches in the Northeast Ohio Master of Fine Arts program (NEOMFA) and is its campus coordinator. He is the author of a book of short fiction, *The Temporary Life,* and his stories, articles, and interviews have been featured in publications such as *Glimmer Train, Poets & Writers Magazine Online, Michigan Quarterly Review, Vermont Literary Review, 10,000 Tons of Black Ink, Oracle, The Helix,* and *Istanbul Literary Review.* His story "He's No Sandy Koufax" won first prize in the thirteenth annual David Dornstein Memorial Creative Writing Contest, and "Brothers," an excerpt from his recently completed novel, *Celluloid Strangers,* was the winner of the 2007 Cervená Barva Press Fiction Chapbook Prize. Wasserman is the founder of *Rubbertop Review,* an annual journal of writing from greater Ohio, and lives in Akron, Ohio, with his wife, Thea, their three cats, and an adorable Saint Bernard mix.

Permissions